Wild Rough Country
Right to Pretty Heroines
Birds

Holly Myers

then/and

© Holly Myers, 2019.
then/and publications
ISBN: 978-1-947322-95-0

Wild Rough Country

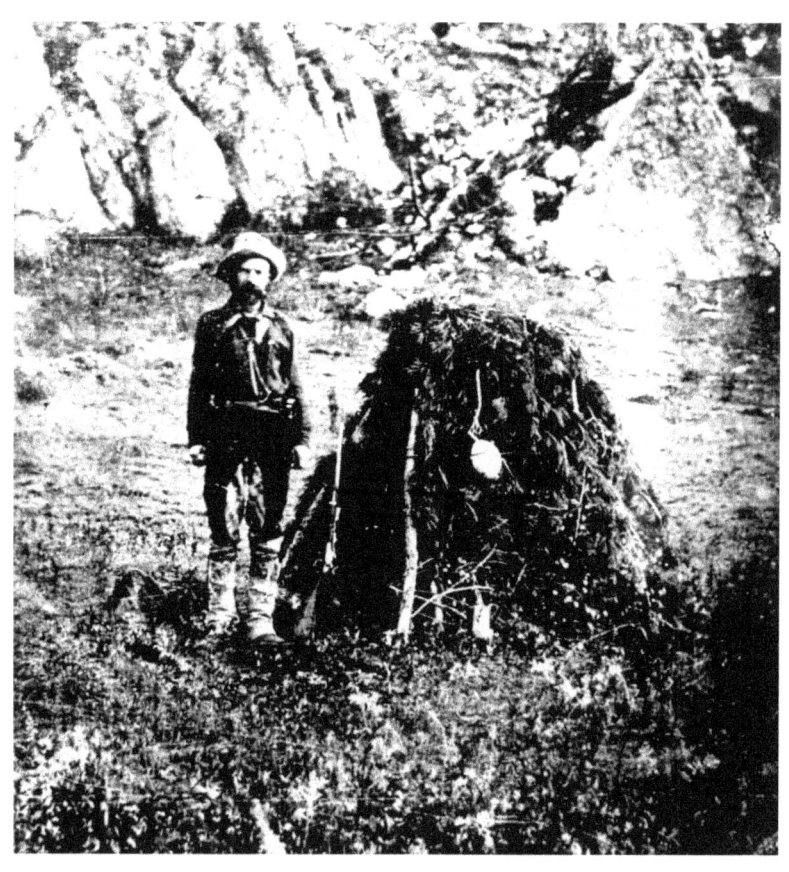

Wild, rough country, rocky ridges, brush-tangled coulees, crisscrossed by trails known only to wild animals that seldom saw any but wilder, warrior neighbors, in a region so big a good fast crow couldn't wing over it in a week—that sort of home ground is bound to encourage outlaw tendencies. It breeds the will to resist, to break away and keep freedom.

—Ike Blassingame

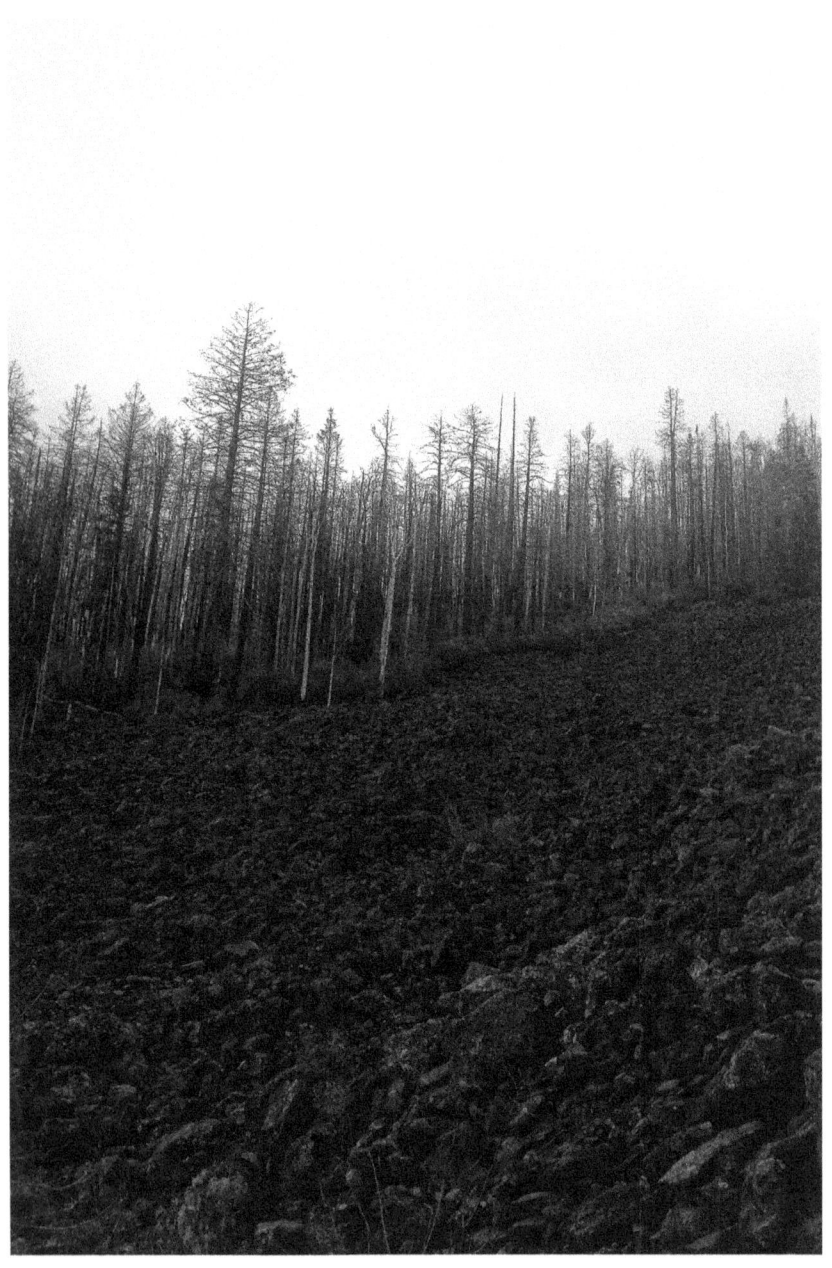

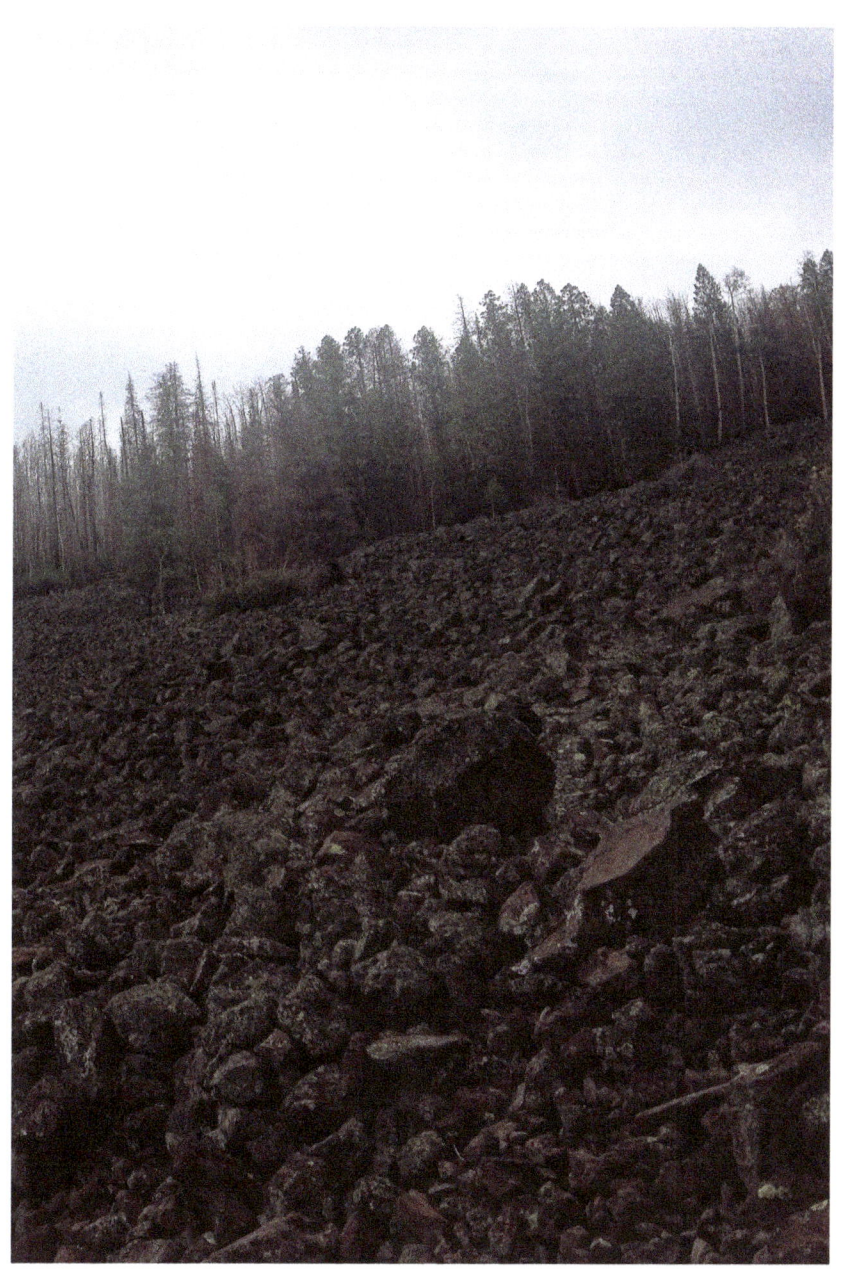

ALBUQUERQUE, NM — Late Sunday night, police say an SUV hauling a U-Haul trailer was stolen outside a Residence Inn in southeast Albuquerque. Inside that trailer was a casket and the body of [an Oklahoma couple's] loved one.

Police say the couple was traveling from Oklahoma to Kirtland, NM, to bury the woman's father. Around 11 a.m. APD says it found the stolen SUV, trailer and casket with the body inside near Gibson and Girard.

APD hasn't arrested anyone for the theft yet, but believe their suspects are already in custody for separate crimes.

SANTA FE, NM — Santa Fe police have arrested a Ramah, NM, man on suspicion of robbery after he was accused of slapping a customer at The Shake Foundation restaurant and then stealing his green chile cheeseburger.

The customer said [the man] first performed a dance, then struck him in the face. The customer also said he felt threatened when [the man] began gripping a belt that [the man] wore around his neck.

An employee of The Shake Foundation told police the hamburger fell to the ground, where [the man] retrieved it. Then he fled.

CLOVIS, NM — Two people were killed and four others were injured when a gunman walked into the Clovis-Carver library Monday afternoon and opened fire. The four who were injured are recovering in a Texas hospital.

Authorities on Tuesday identified the two deceased victims—[a] 61-year-old [woman] and [a] 48-year-old [woman]. Both women worked at the library.

The teenage boy accused in the deadly shooting had been in trouble at school, had recently contemplated suicide and had "anxiety attacks" that resulted in his going home from church on Sunday morning, his pastors said.

[The boy] was arrested without incident after police said he opened fire a little after 4 p.m. Monday in the library.

Pastors at Clovis' Living Word Church of God said the shooting stunned them because they thought [the boy] was making positive strides in recent weeks, following what both described as a "very hard life."

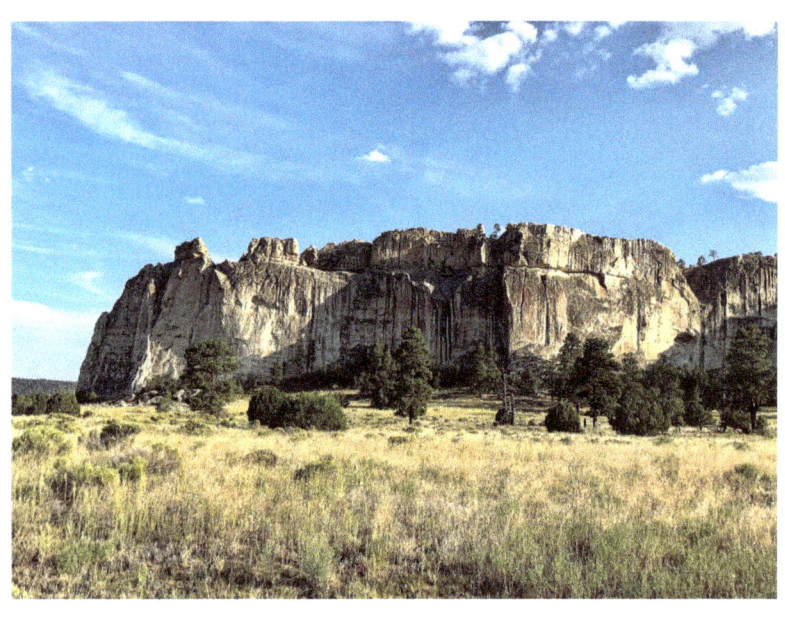

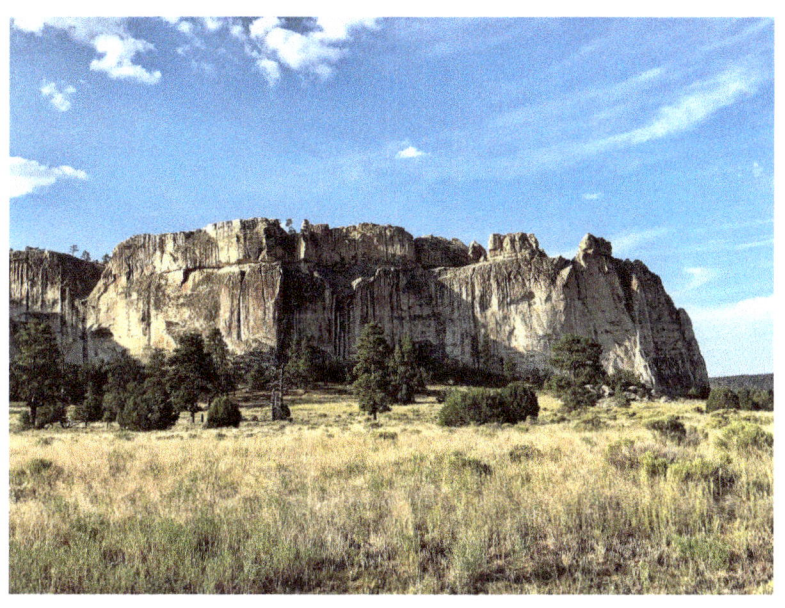

EAGLE, CO — Authorities say a man who was in a Colorado court for violating his bond on a drug charge is in even more trouble after a wad of cocaine fell from his hat while he was in front of the judge.

The *Vail Daily* reported Wednesday that [the] 43-year-old [man] was standing next to two other defendants at an Eagle County District Court podium when he took his hat off and a square of folded paper fell out. A police officer watched the paper filled with cocaine fall to the floor, and after reviewing surveillance footage, authorities determined it fell from [the man's] hat.

[The man] was then walked to the county jail. He was charged with narcotics possession and another bond violation.

GREELEY, CO — A Greeley man could face felony charges after police say he stole three different vehicles one August night and finally drove away in a dump truck naked.

According to affidavits made recently public, [the man], 54, told Weld County sheriff's deputies that on the night of Aug. 15, he was "running from people for 6-7 hours." While he was on the run, he snuck into the garage of a home on Weld County Road 13, just south of Platteville. While inside, police believe, he found some tater tots in a refrigerator, cooked them in the garage microwave and ate them. He then stole the 2002 Chevrolet Duramax inside.

[The man] did not, apparently, get far in the truck, because it was found crashed in an irrigation ditch at about 4:30 a.m. Aug. 16. Police found [the man's] soaked clothes inside.

Although [the man] was naked, he kept running. He appeared on [a] 71-year-old [resident's] doorstep on Weld 28 in the Platteville area, the report stated. He asked [the resident] for clothes, but [the resident] refused and told him to leave.

After [the resident] shut the door, he heard the diesel engine of his 2002 Chevrolet Sierra, and when he looked outside, he saw the truck beginning to move. He ran outside and began to struggle with [the man] to get him out of the Sierra.

[The man] later told police [the resident] did actually pull him out of the truck, but it careened over a bank into a pond on the property.

It didn't stop him, though. He ran down a hill to a dump truck [the resident] had nearby. [The man] found the keys in the truck and drove away.

Somewhere along the line, he was able to find some clothes, he told police, and he drove the dump truck to American Demolition in Brighton, where he worked.

Police later found the dump truck abandoned nearby.

Officers only recently learned about the thefts while interviewing [the man] in the Weld County Jail while he was held on suspicion of an unrelated forgery charge.

LAKEWOOD, CO — A 15-year-old boy from Lakewood has been arrested on suspicion of first-degree murder in the deadly stabbing of an adult woman in Longmont, police said Sunday.

Longmont Police responded to The Shores at McIntosh Lake apartments just after 6 p.m. Saturday after getting reports of a disturbance in the area. At the apartment complex, police found an injured woman who was taken to Longmont United Hospital where she later died.

[A resident] who lives at the complex said he heard commotion outside his door and found the victim, who had multiple stab wounds, covered in blood on the second-floor breezeway. "I saw a girl lying at the bottom of the stair steps. I screamed out to her, 'Are you ok?' She didn't answer so I ran up to her. I saw that she was bleeding," he said.

As he assisted the woman, [the resident] said he saw the suspect—wearing all black and a motorcycle helmet—walk down from the third-floor holding what he said looked like a folding knife.

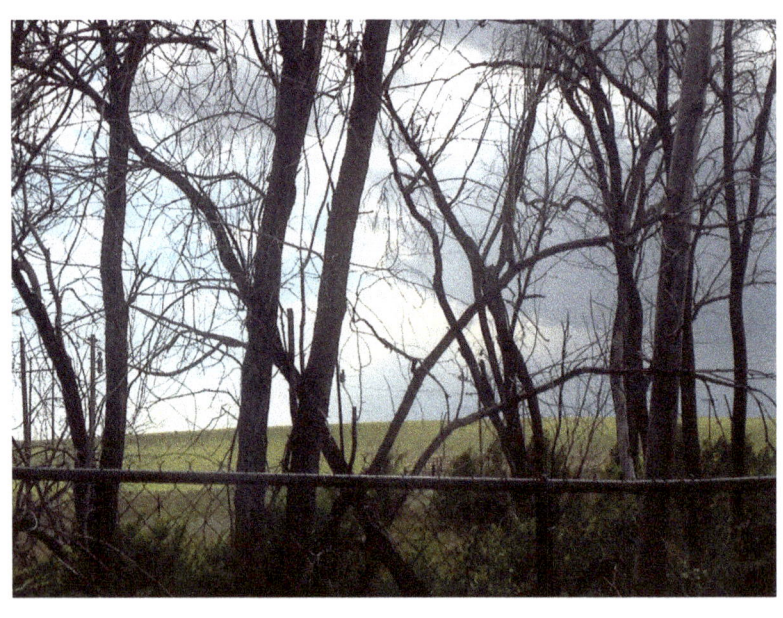

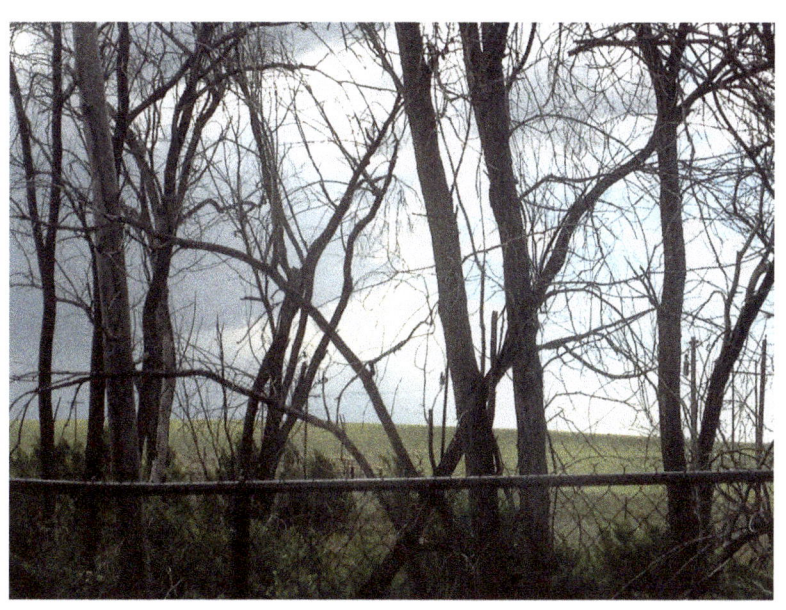

PIERRE, SD — [A man from] Pierre told [a judge] on Tuesday he had been driving drunk on Sept. 5 coming back to Pierre from Fort Pierre.

"Very, very drunk," said [the man], who is 30.

Exactly how drunk, [the judge] asked during [the man's] hearing in court.

"Four two four," [the man] said, meaning 0.424 percent blood alcohol content (BAC), or more than five times the legal drunk driving limit of 0.08 percent.

"That is very, very high," [the judge] said. "Is that a common occurrence for you?"

"No," [the man] said.

"Tell me, back on September 5, how you came to be arrested driving that drunk," [the judge] said.

"It's my understanding I left [an establishment in Fort Pierre] ... I wanted to go home," [the man] said. "I got across the bridge and got surprised by three police [vehicles]. Somebody had called me in for drinking and driving."

"Had you been drinking?"

"Yes, your honor."

SIOUX FALLS, SD — A 22-year-old Sioux Falls man faces terrorist threat charges after yelling at a group of people that he was going to kill them inside a business Saturday night.

The man walked into a business on South Sycamore Avenue Saturday and started pointing and yelling at people, saying he was going to kill them and they were going to die, said a police spokesman.

There were about 15 to 20 people who ran from the store, but nobody was hurt.

"They were obviously in fear for their lives," [the police spokesman] said.

[The man] tried to re-enter the business but employees prevented him from doing so. Police found him walking north on Sycamore Avenue. He did not have any weapons.

RAPID CITY, SD — A Rapid City teenager accused of killing a convenience store clerk during a January robbery has pleaded guilty to second-degree murder.

[The boy] was 17 but was charged as an adult. He's now 18.

Authorities say [the boy] and [a] 19-year-old [friend] killed the 45-year-old [woman] as they tried to steal beer from a Loaf 'N Jug store. [The boy] was accused of stabbing [the woman] more than three dozen times.

[The boy] said in court he had used medicine, marijuana and alcohol, and blacked out and doesn't remember what happened.

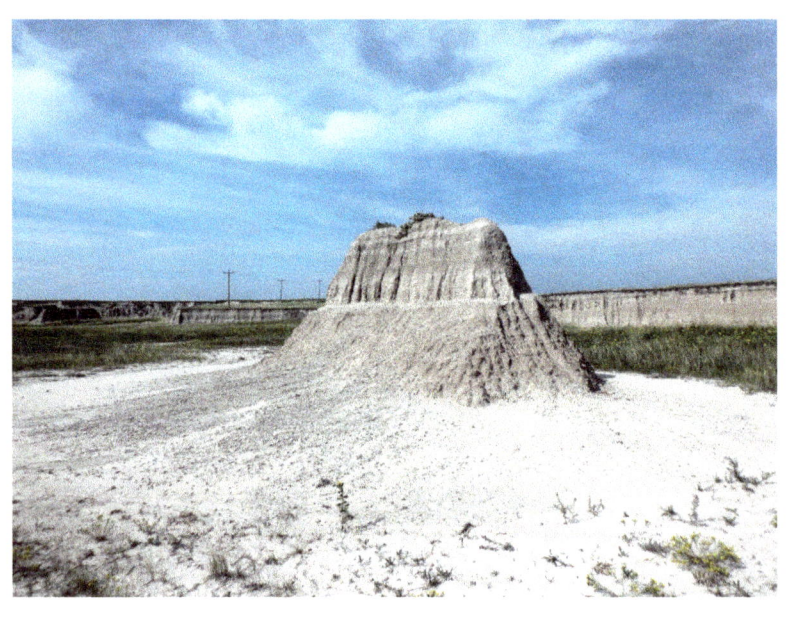

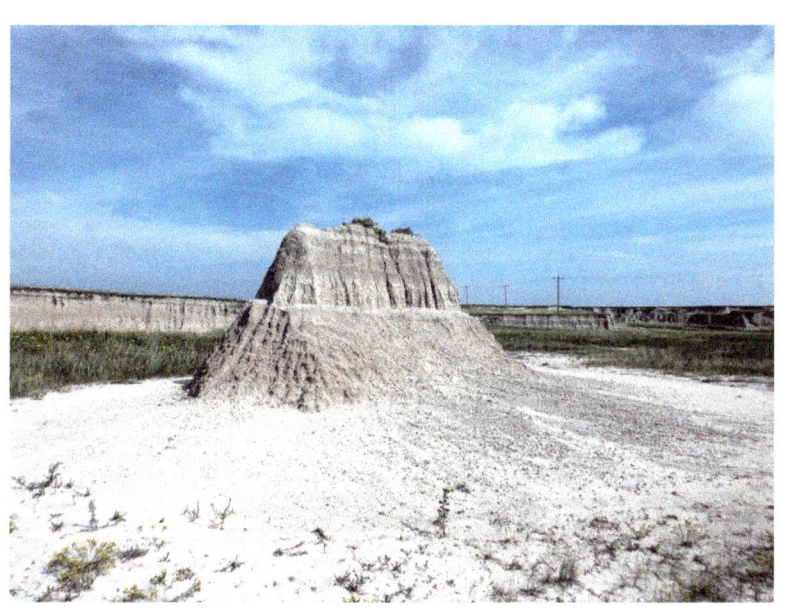

A two-lane highway channels into a four-lane no man's land toward Main Street. Wide, empty medians. A confusion of frontage roads. At the Family Dollar, a young woman stands alone in line with a bag of Cheetos and a child's t-shirt on a hanger that reads "My Day Begins At Noon" in pink glitter letters. The sky is a hard, winter gray; the temperature is down twenty degrees or more, with wind. A woman pulls at a hatchback door against the wind, hair whipping across her thick face. A miscellany of dim establishments and weeds: a tax service, a truck repair, auto parts, tacos, a drivetrain specialist, a county health office, a liquor store. A church in a warehouse with a swingset outside. The dark gray of asphalt and the light gray of sidewalk. Light poles and electrical lines. The bridge arcs over the vast, striated railyard. A gray stucco motel with a brown shingle roof floats on a parking lot with four cars. "MOTEL"—just "MOTEL"—in big red block letters on a white sign.

Cold wind through the parking lot. A 1992 silver Toyota with a car seat in back, with Hello Kitty hanging from the rear view mirror. A 2012 black Acura with tinted windows moving slow, snake-like and inscrutible.

St. Joseph's Hospital Emergency Room, Phoenix, 1 a.m.:

And you're aware that you're talking weird?
Have you ever been diagnosed with a mental illness?
Do you have a history of seizures?
Because you're on seizure meds.
You're homeless now?

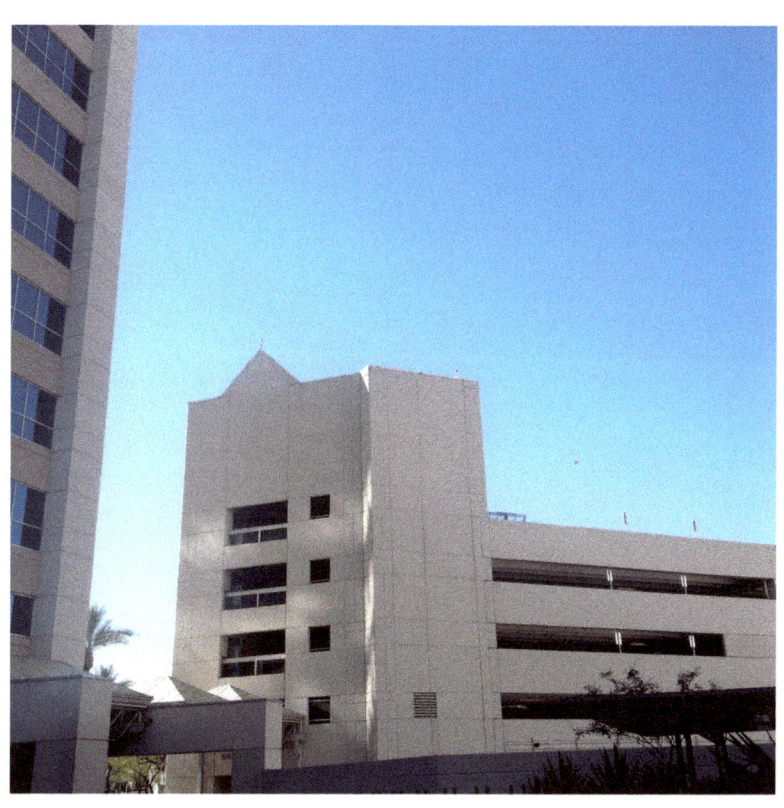

Court documents filled with leering security guards; that story told again and again. Guards who watch you through the camera. Guards who trap you in small rooms with filthy talk and lewd exhibitions. Guards who text you unwanted pictures. Guards who brush against you down narrow passageways then cut your shifts when you complain. Guards alone with you through long hours, often the loneliest hours, while your kids are sleeping.

Crimes committed in Walmart parking lots. Shots fired. A stunted kind of yelling. A security guard holds a black man down unjustly. A screeching of tires. A young woman with a baby yelling obscenities. A young man running, pants flapping. The hard thump of tires up over a curb in a panic. Shots fired into a car. Elderly couples pause in the doorway. A car alarm. The lights of a police car running red across a cinderblock wall in the darkness and the stillness of a man, a woman in uniform with notepads. Red lights circle a tawdry perimeter, asphalt and an upturned shopping cart. A young man on the ground in a private world of pain that no one else has any part of.

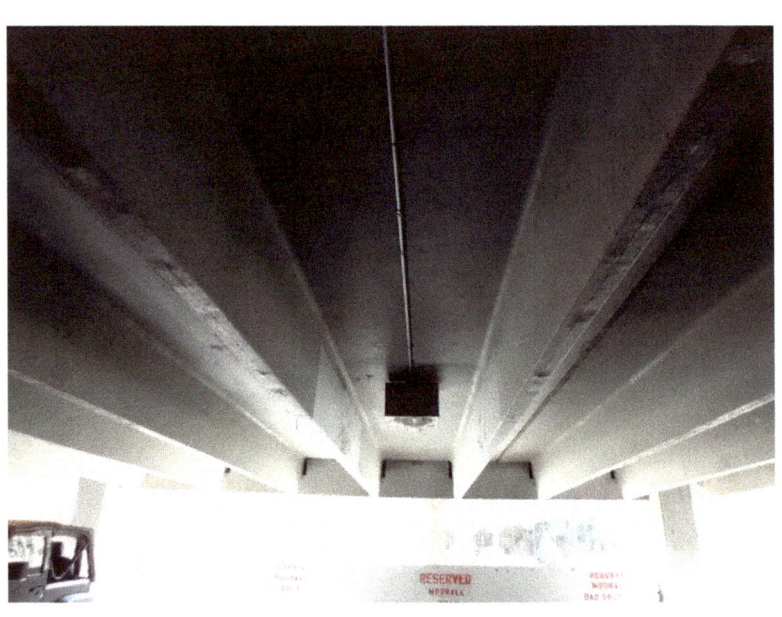

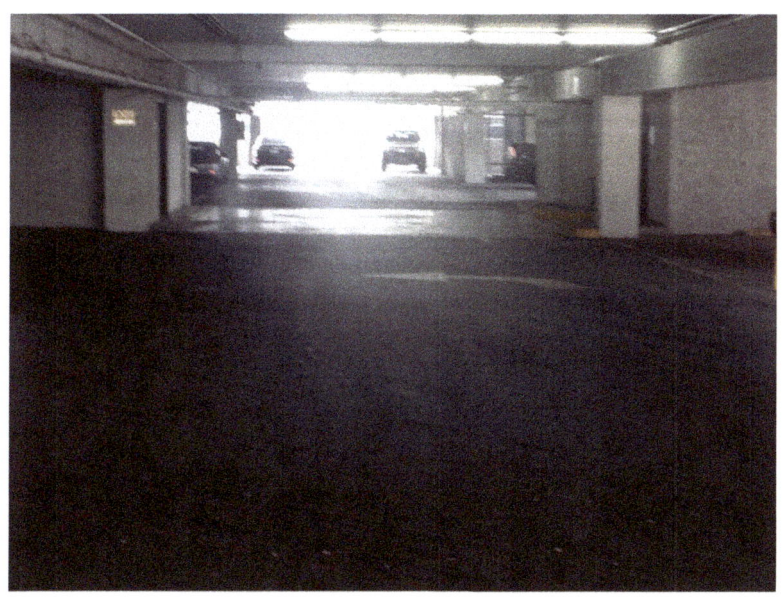

Red sweatshirt, red sweatpants, red baseball cap, white sneakers, neck tattoos.

The Lariat Motel sign is filled with bullet holes. A bow legged cowboy with a lasso grins forever, his face shot away, eyes crooked.

A sign in the shape of an ice cream cone, tilted on its armature.

A Thai restaurant in a cowboy town.

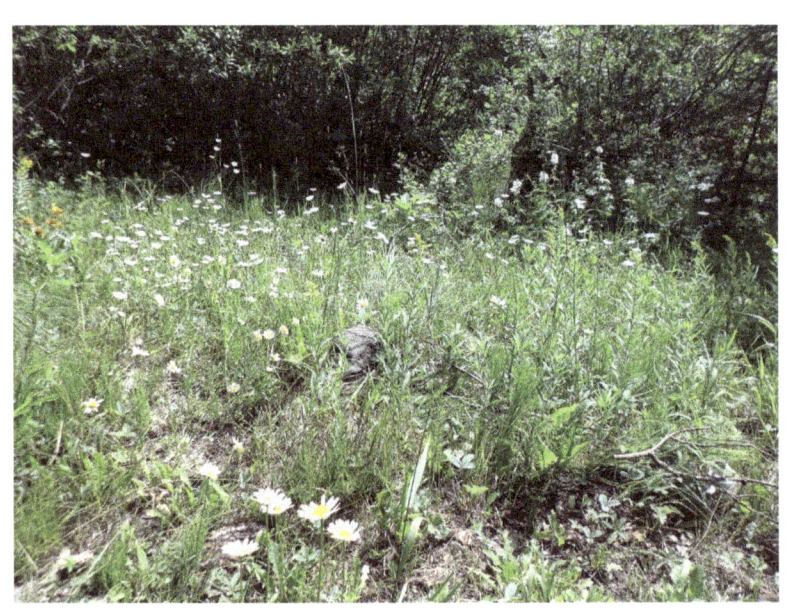

DURANGO, CO — A human remains detection dog searched [the man's] house Aug. 5 for the scent of a corpse. The dog, Molly, indicated the presence of cadaver scent in various locations of the home, including the living room and the washing machine.

"These are indications of the presence of a large source of human remains," the indictment says.

Also that month, Molly indicated a cadaver scent on [the man's] clothes that he reportedly wore the night of Nov. 18.

The cadaver dog also searched [the man's] Dodge pickup and alerted to the presence of a cadaver scent in several locations, including the bed of the truck.

Commerce in parking lots among waning Winnebagos and vans. Buicks packed to the roof. Old and new pick up trucks. Men sloped of shoulder and shadowy at a distance, yet there must be jokes there, and goals, and threats, and emotions. There's laughter from around the side of the truck, three or four men who prefer the open air to a room with only a single window at the front. The smell of cigarette smoke. Joking about co-workers. Joking about women. Repeating the jokes of other men. There was a fire on the premises then it was all condemned, a blight on the gateway of our fine city.

"Missing Cheyenne man found dead near Laramie"

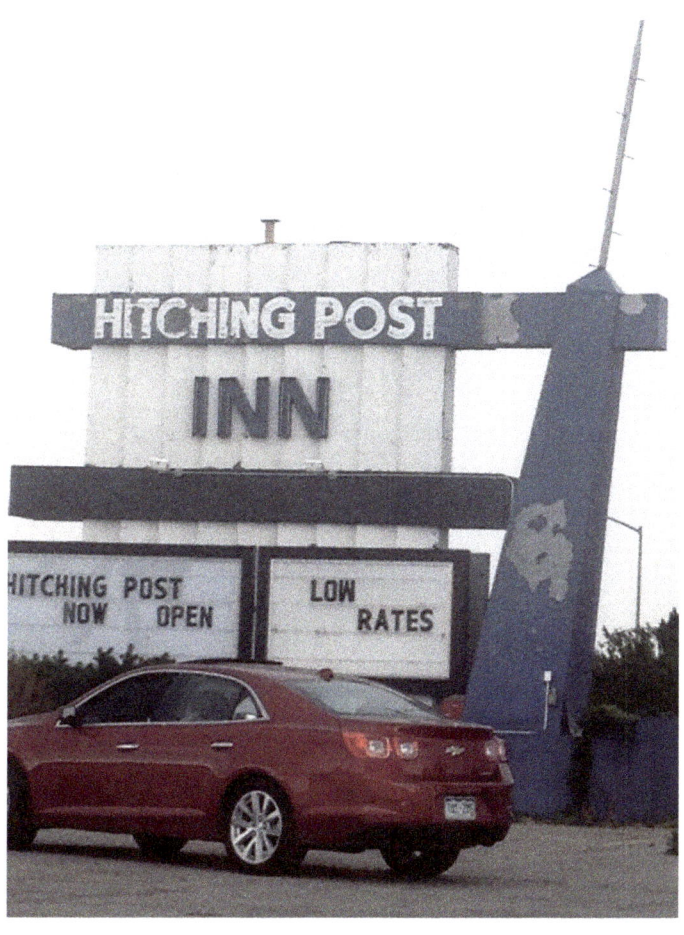

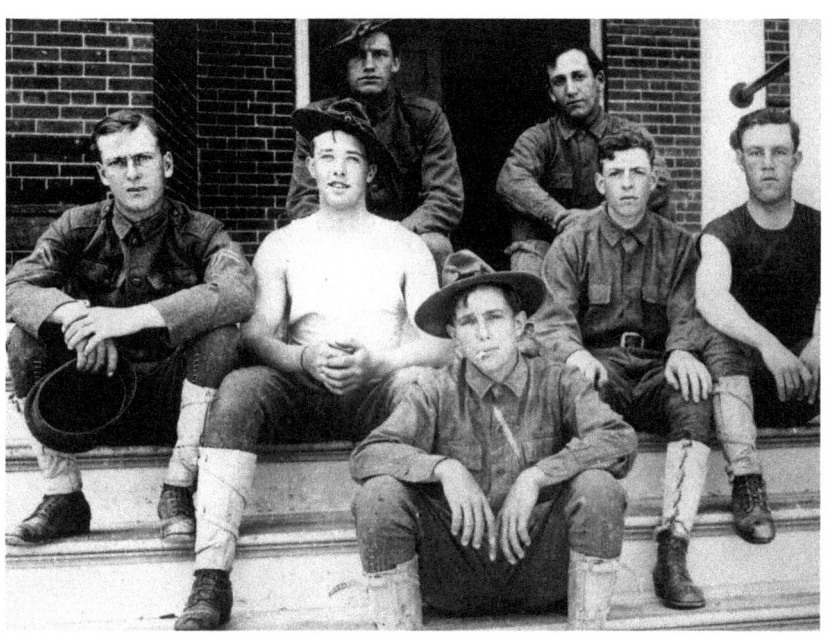

KENNEBEC, NE — A Vivian man whose infant daughter died from head trauma and brain injuries pleaded guilty to first-degree manslaughter on Thursday morning.

When asked to provide an account of what happened on May 4, 2017, [the man] responded only to questions from his attorney.

[The man] indicated that on that date, he and his daughter had been alone in the home. He had tried to throw his daughter into a bassinet, and he said that he was unsure of whether or not her head hit a dresser when he threw her.

"There was a possibility, but I wasn't sure," [the man] said when asked if his actions led to the infant's death.

Crimes committed on custody visits. AMBER ALERT: a 1992 Ford Taurus, tan. A boy boards a plane from Pennsylvania to Colorado; he doesn't want to go. *Mom, you don't understand, he's*—a scrap of a hat found in the woods. A court order. AMBER ALERT: a 2014 Toyota Forerunner, black. Children in cars across great American distances at night, state lines like threads, like trip wires. No, he's my son, it's ok, he's just upset. Are they crying? Gas stations and fast food restaurants. Candy bars. The man is a prominent figure in the town. For nearly a year, he grieves in public. Another man is an insurance salesman. Young bodies, familiar bodies of like DNA, crumpled in the dirt, gone out. This man confesses, but they could be anywhere. A thousand miles! He doesn't even know. There was a dirt pile, maybe, and an overpass. Here, the man is a construction worker. Two children by birth and two by marriage. Mothers left gazing eastward from the west, or westward from the east, helpless. You don't *remember*? A boy and a girl limp in a car in a locked garage. A girl tangled up in the dirt. The weight of the dirt. That first horrific shovelful. AMBER ALERT: a 2009 Honda Civic, silver. Children, faultless. If I can't have them, no one will.

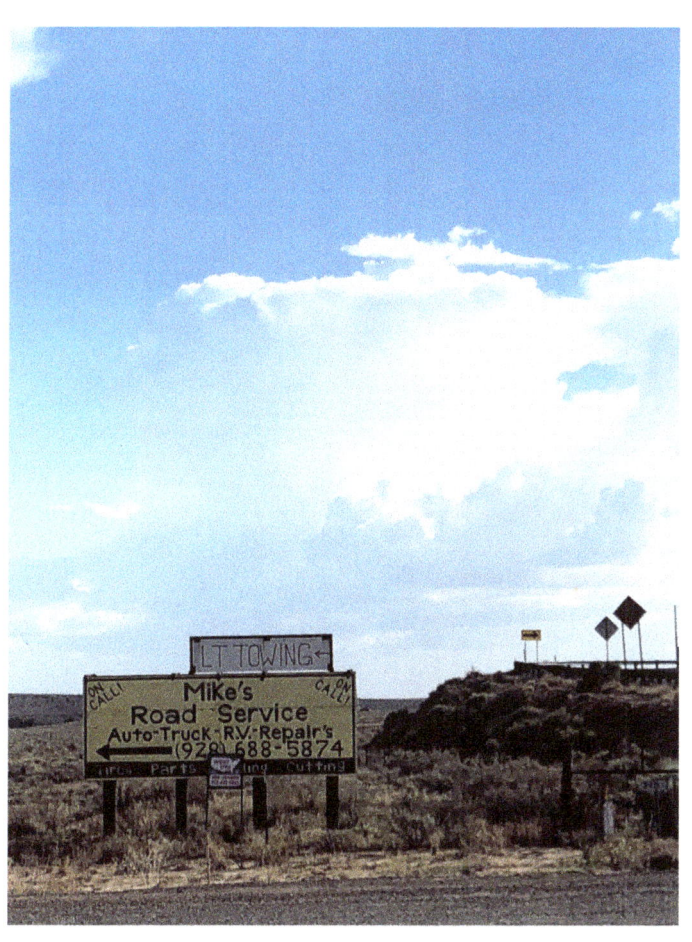

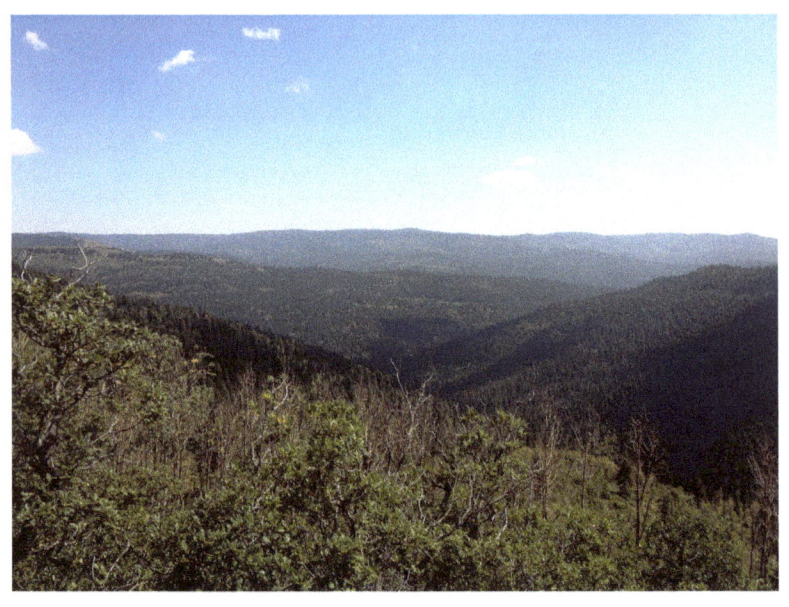

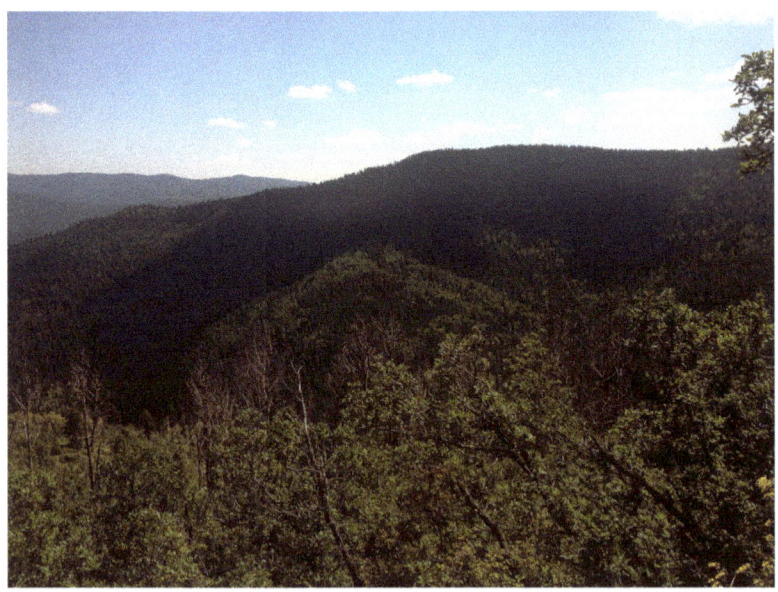

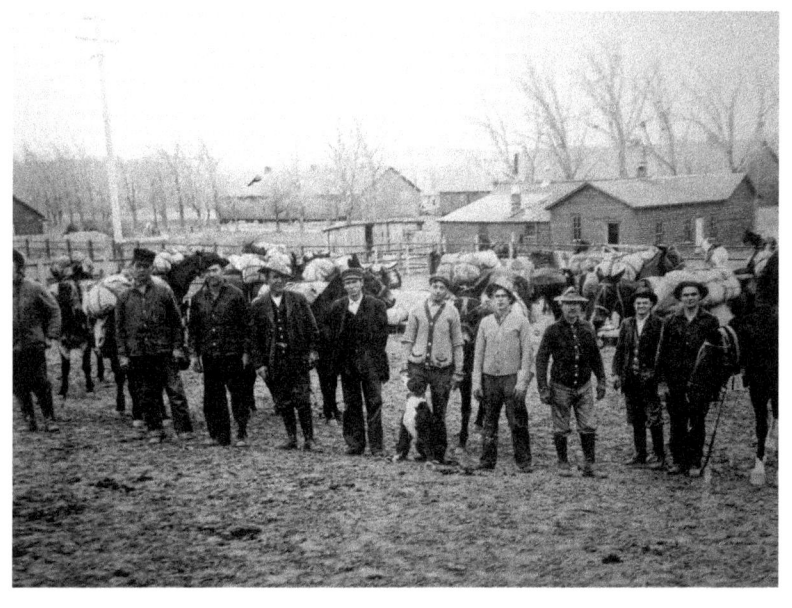

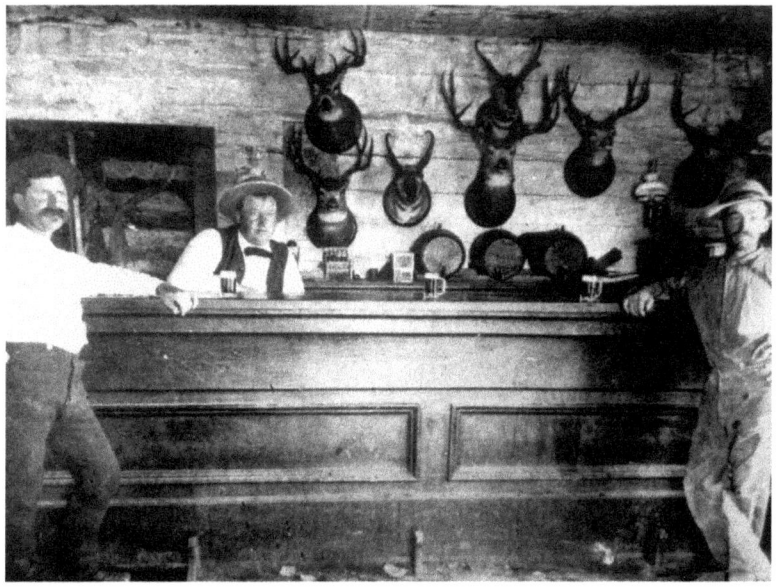

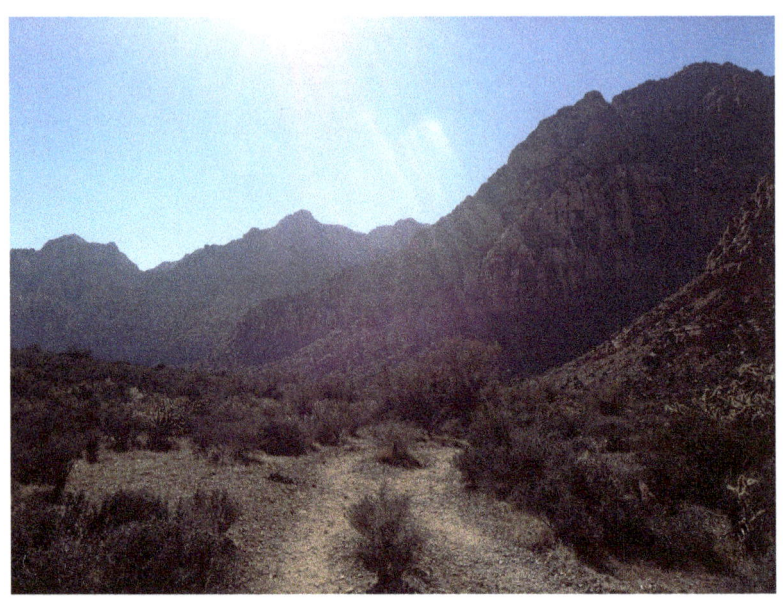

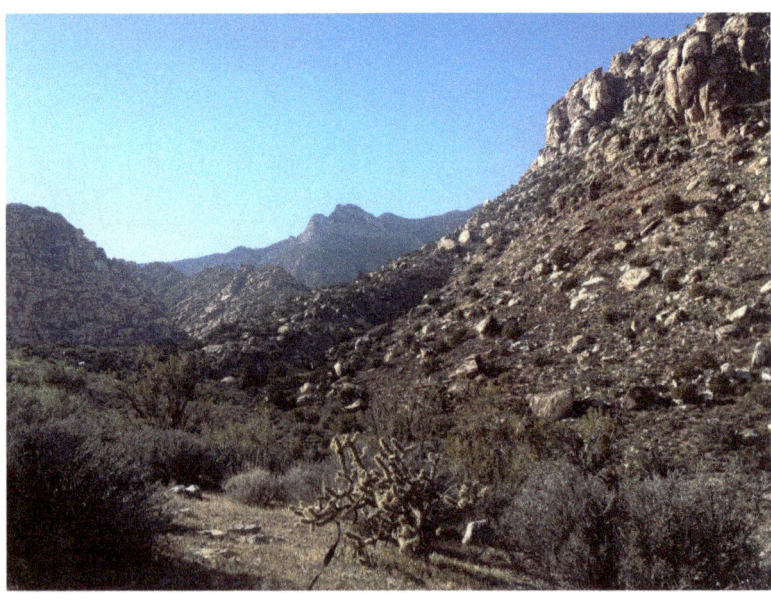

> I kept on runnin'
> Into the southlands
> That's where they found me
> My head in my hands
> The sheriff he asked me
> Why had I run?
> And then it came to me
> Just what I had done
> And all for no reason
> Just one piece of lead
> I hung my head
> I hung my head
>
> —Johnny Cash

Right to Pretty Heroines

NOTE ON THE TEXT

The text on the following pages is drawn from the notebooks of F. Scott Fitzgerald, as compiled by Edmund Wilson in *The Crack Up*, published shortly after Fitzgerald's death in 1940. The notebooks were a collection of fragments—notes, observations and pieces of past stories saved for possible re-use—all originally type-written by secretaries and arranged by category in two binders. Many, though not all, of the passages reproduced here come from the section titled "Descriptions of Girls." Most appear in the notebooks exactly as they do here; in one or two cases, I have extracted a portion of a longer passage for the purposes of emphasis or clarity. The title—*Right to Pretty Heroines*—is also taken from the notebooks.

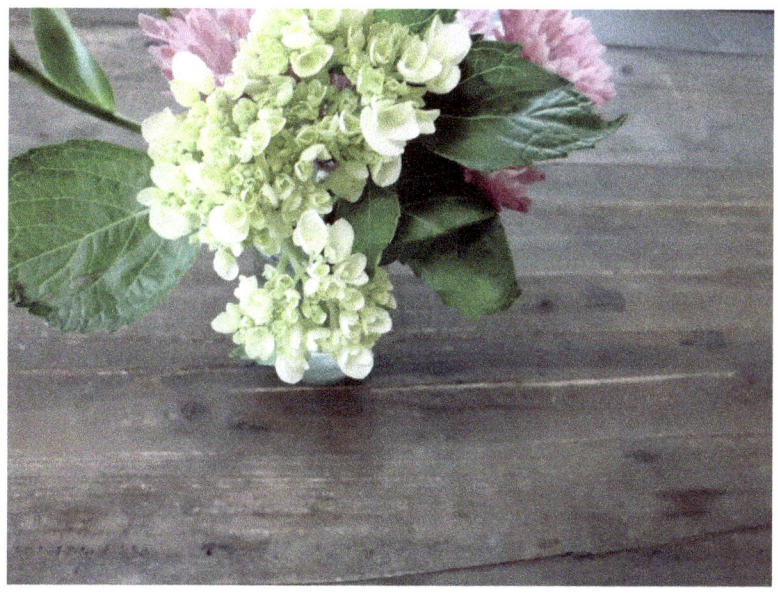

A beauty that had reached the point where it seemed to contain in itself the secret of its own growth, as if it would go on increasing forever.

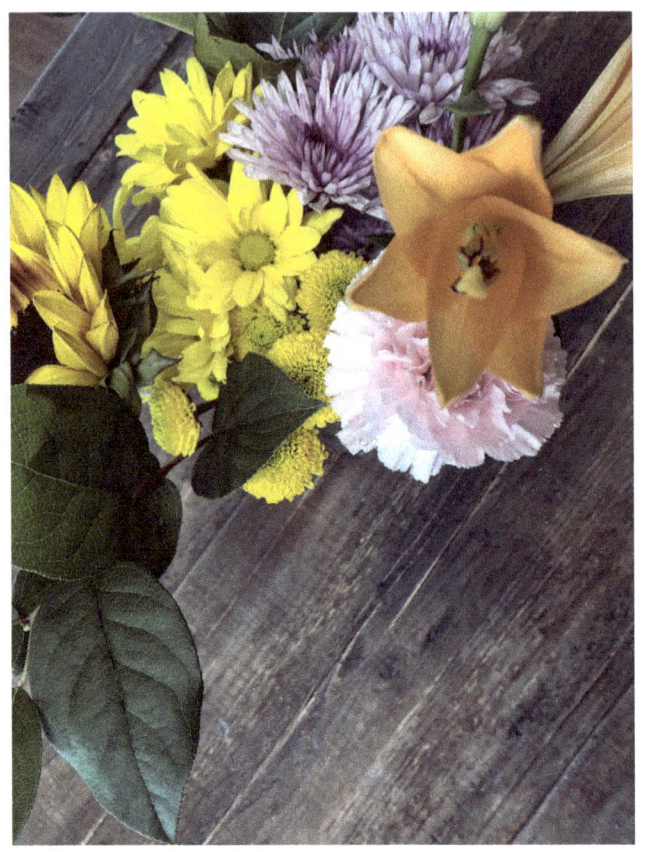

Passing within the radius of the girl's perfume.

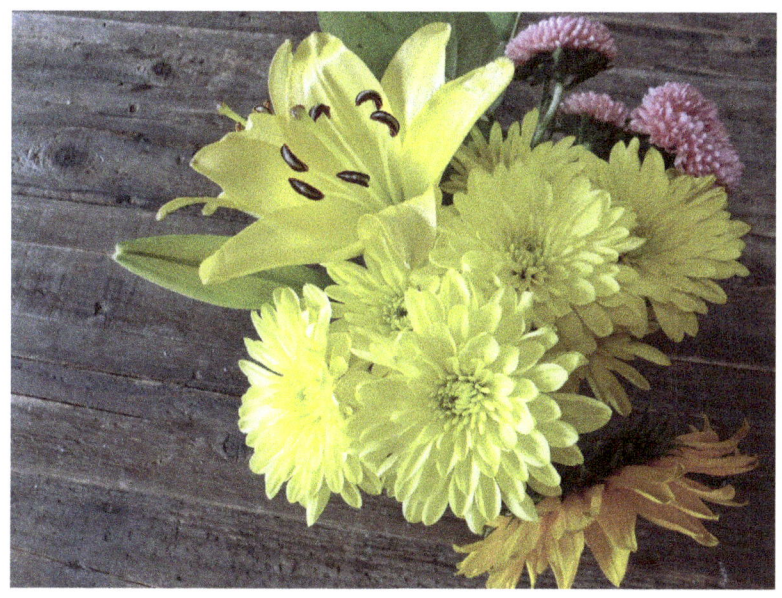

The little fourteen-year-old nymph in the Vagabonds.

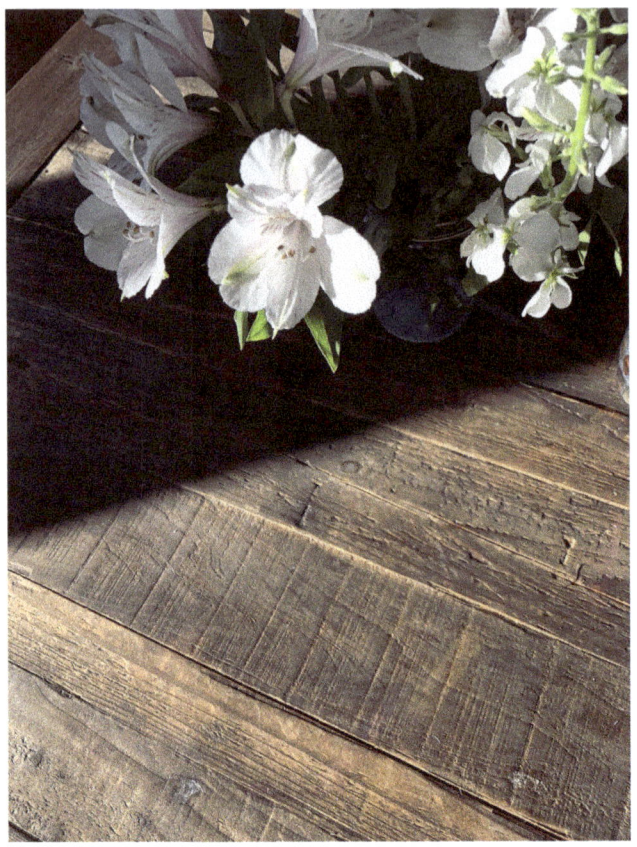

Lola Shisbe had never wrecked a railroad in her life. But she was just sixteen and you had only to look at her to know that her destructive period was going to begin any day now.

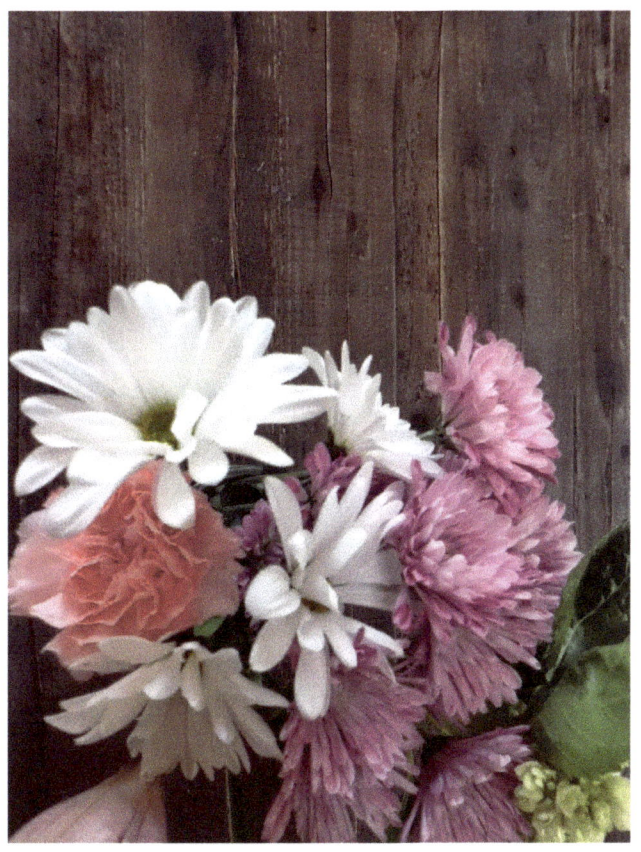

Her childish beauty was wistful and sad about being so rich and sixteen.

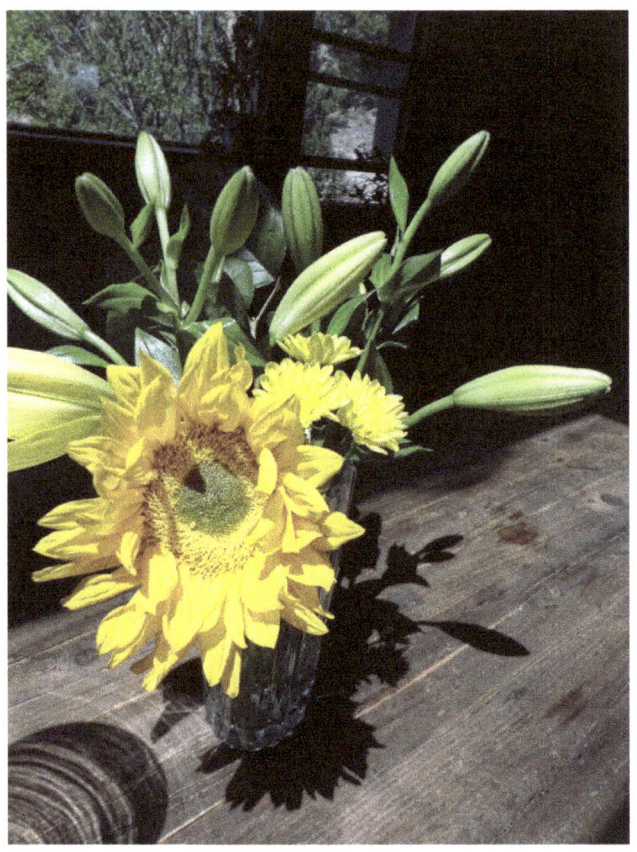

She was a dark, pretty girl with a figure that would be full-blown sooner than she wished. She was just eighteen.

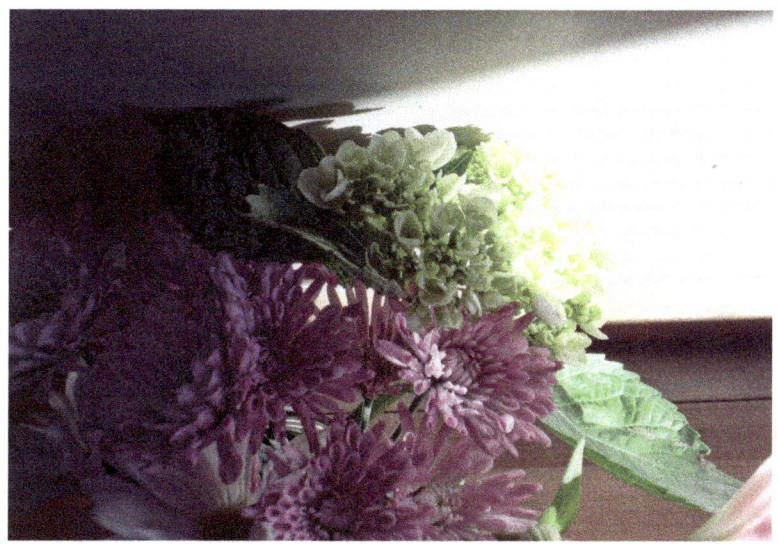

She was not more than eighteen—a dark little beauty with the fine crystal gloss over her that, in brunettes, takes the place of a blonde's bright glow.

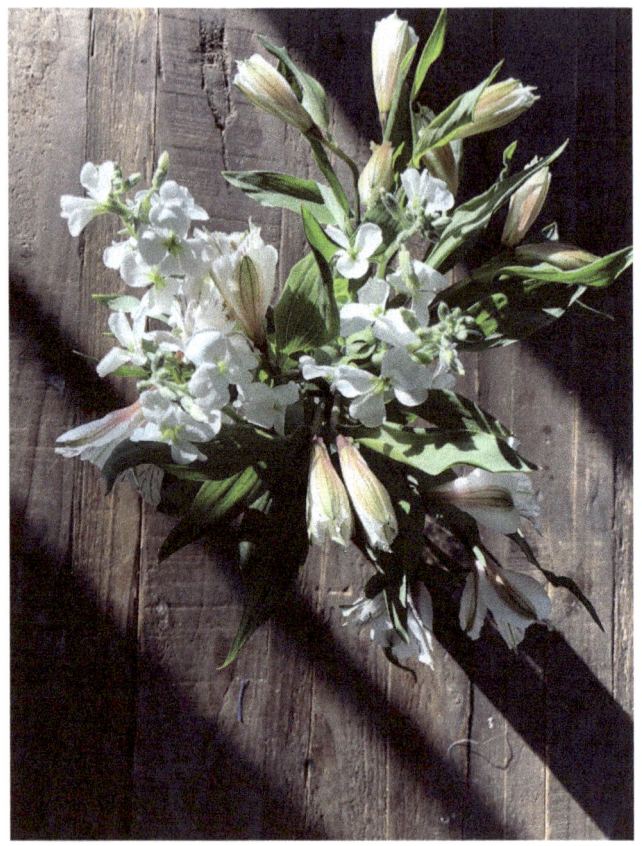

She was eighteen, with such a skin as the Italian painters of the decadence used for corner angels, and all the wishing in the world glistened in her grey eyes.

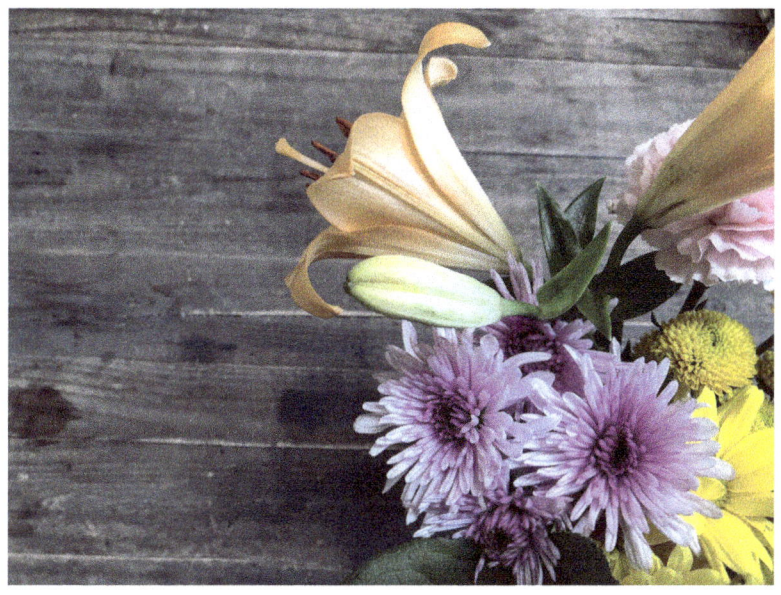

Becky was nineteen, a startling little beauty, with her head set upon her figure as though it had been made separately and then placed there with the utmost precision.

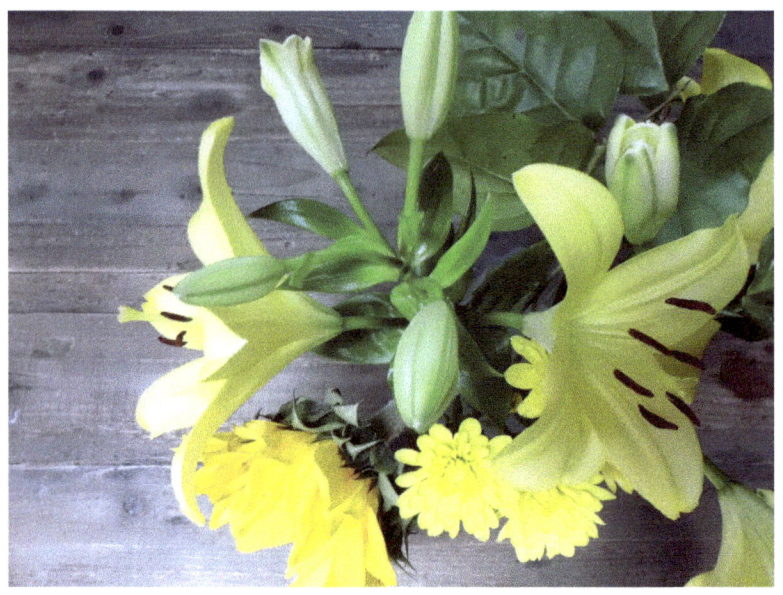

She was a stalk of ripe corn, but bound not as cereals are but as a rare first edition, with all the binder's art. She was lovely and expensive, and about nineteen.

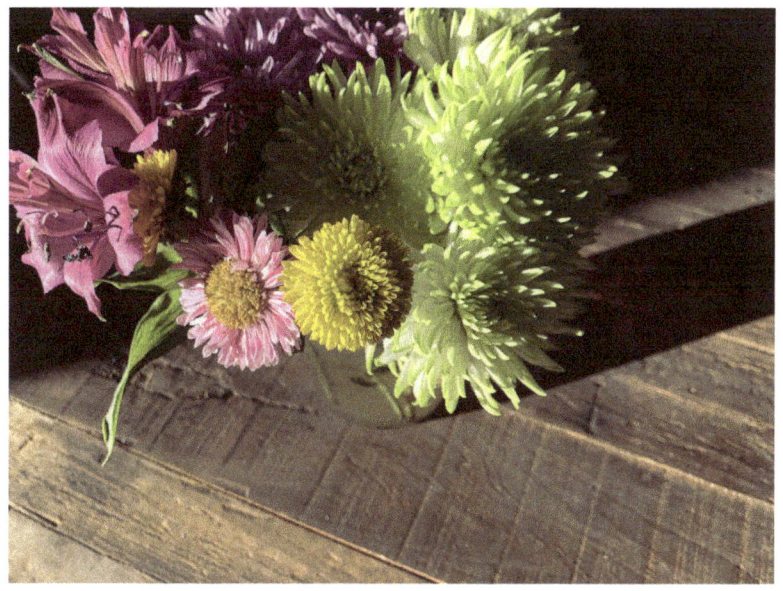

He had not realized that flashing fairness could last so far into the twenties.

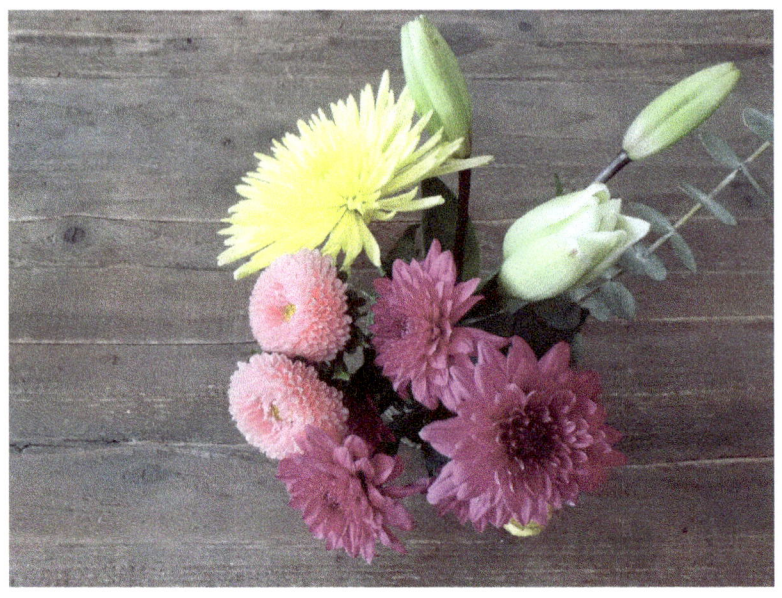

Standing at the gate with that faint glow behind her, Dinah was herself the garden's last outpost, its most representative flower.

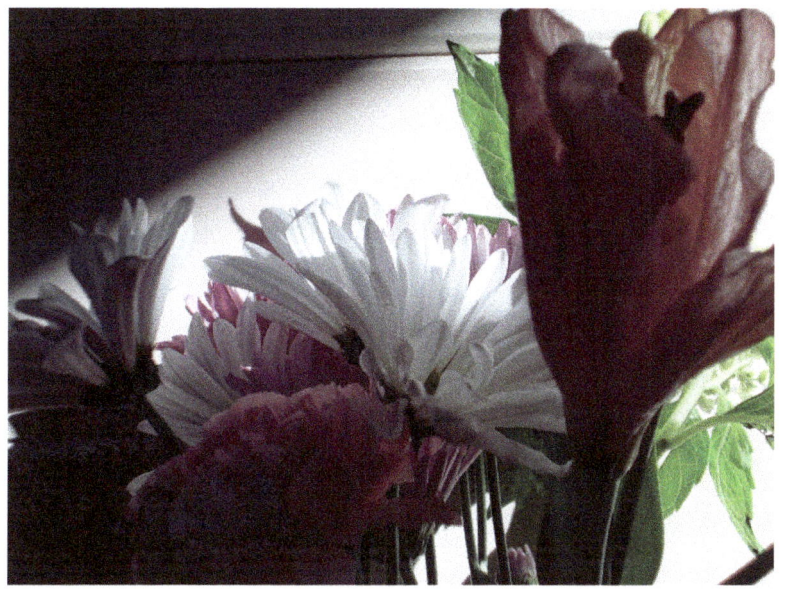

He had passed the wire to her, to a white rose blooming without reason at the end of a cross-bar on the edge of space and time like a newly created tree.

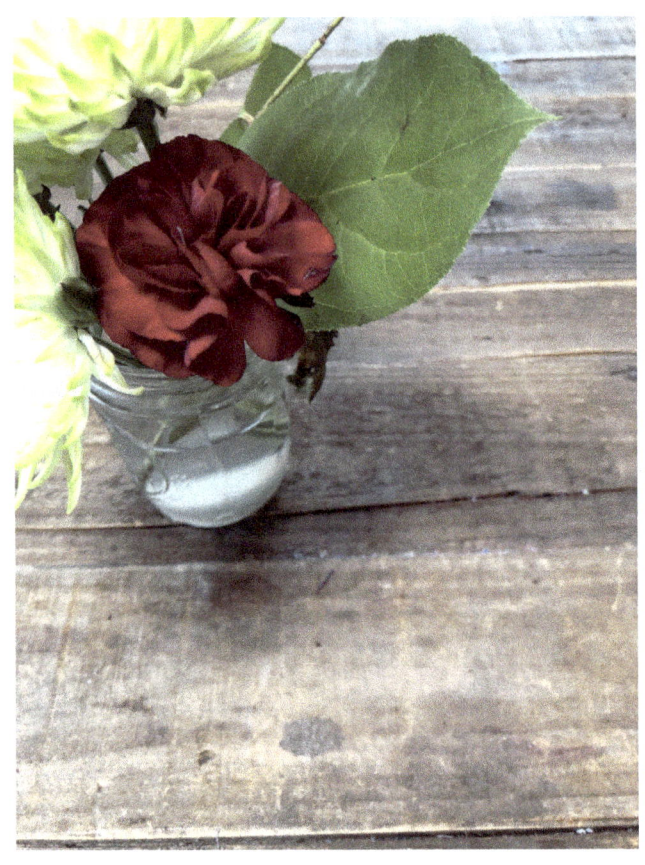

Her beauty was as poised and secure as a flower on a strong stem; her voice was cool and sure, with no wayward instruments in it that played on his emotions.

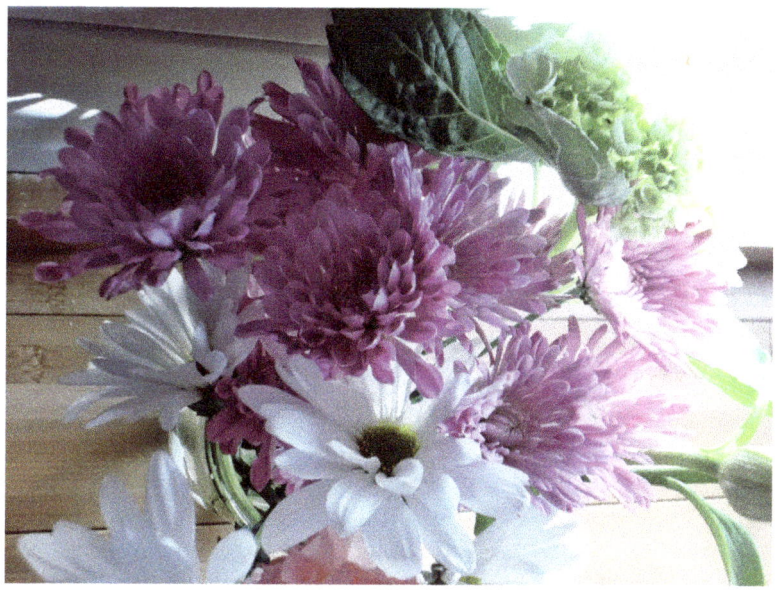

Her face, flushed with cold and then warmed again with the dance, was a riot of lovely, delicate pinks, like many carnations, rising in many shades from the white of her nose to the high spot of her cheeks. Her breathing was very young as she came close to him—young and eager and exciting.

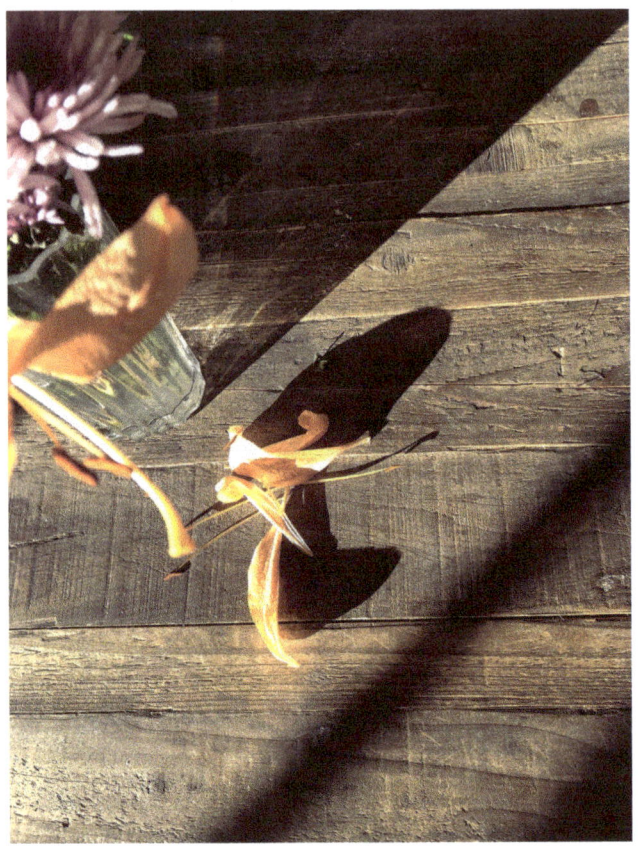

Her mouth was made of two small intersecting cherries pointing off into a bright smile.

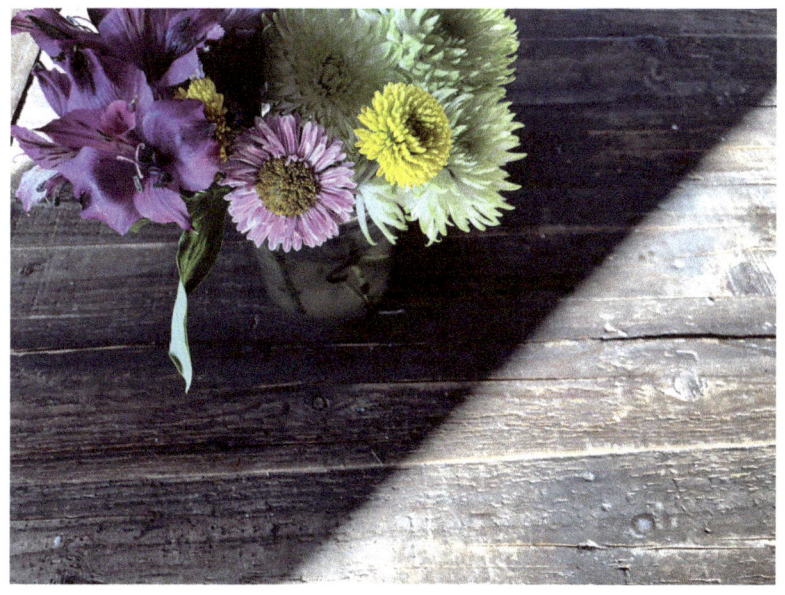

She was a ripe grape, ready to fall for the mere shaking of a vine.

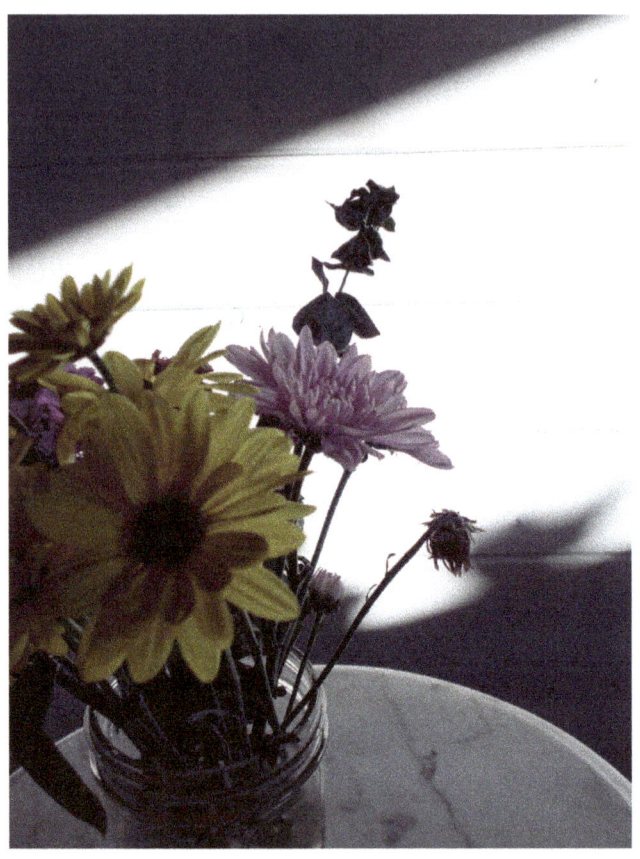

She was the tongue of flame that made the firelight vivid.

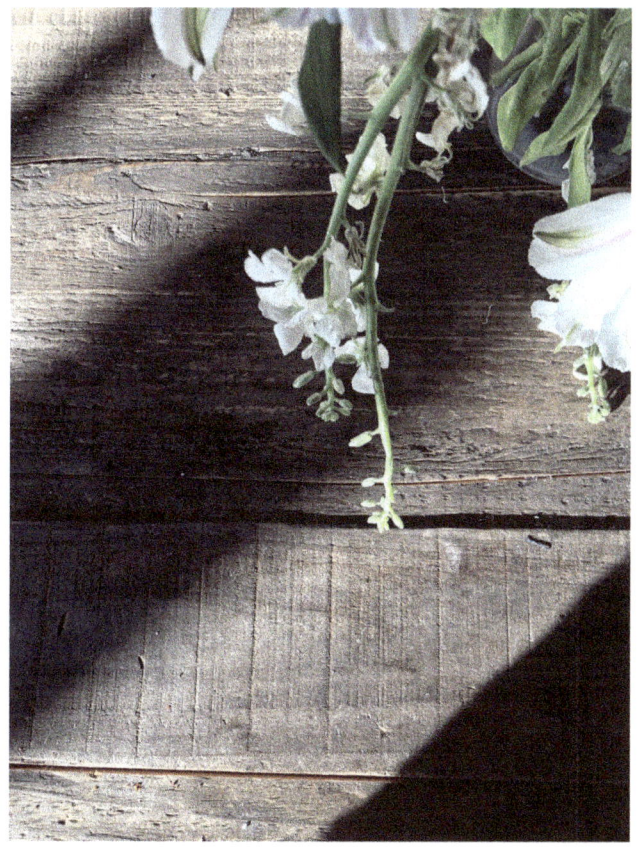

She was a thin burning flame, colorless yet fresh. Her smile came first slowly, shy and bold, as if all the life of that little body had gathered for a moment around her mouth and the rest of her was a wisp that the least wind would blow away. She was a changeling whose lips were the only point of contact with reality.

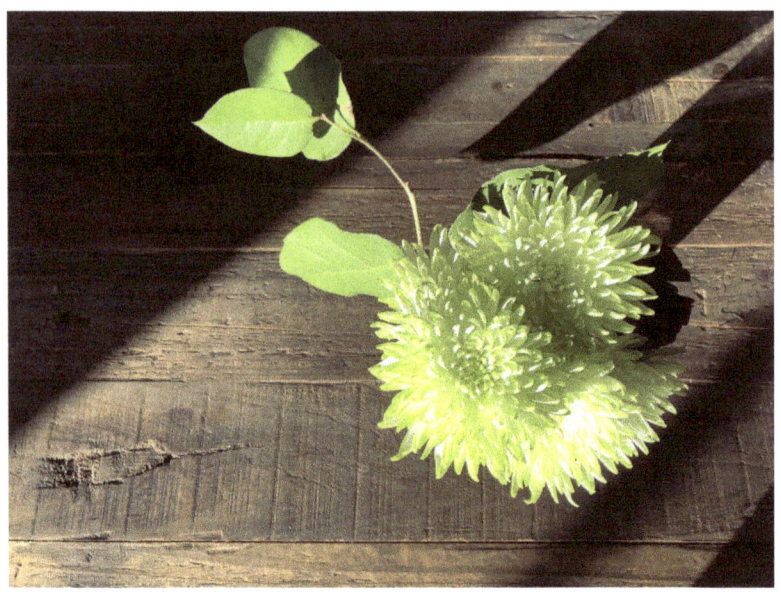

He had thought of her once as a bubble and had told her about it—an iridescent soap-blown bubble with a thin delicate film over all the colors of the rainbow. He had stopped abruptly at that point but he was conscious, too, of the sun panning gold from the clear brooks of her hair, of her tawny skin—hell! he had to stop thinking of such things.

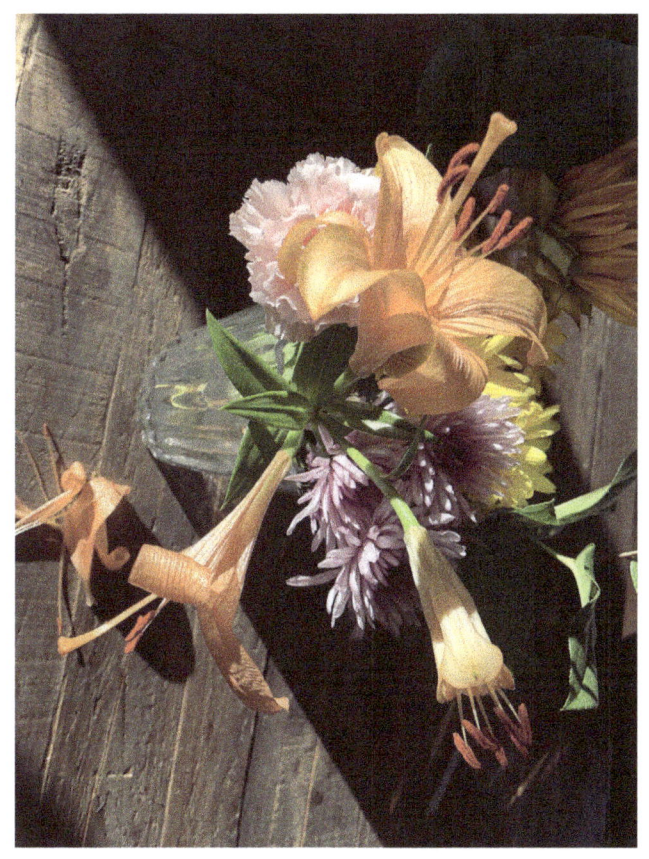

She was a key-board all resonant and gleaming.

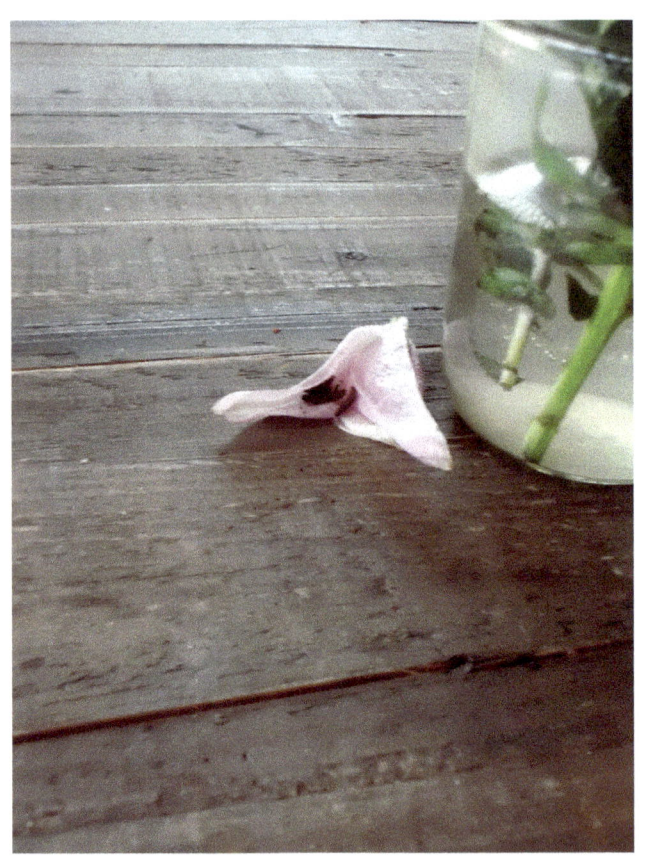

* * * * looks like a trinket.

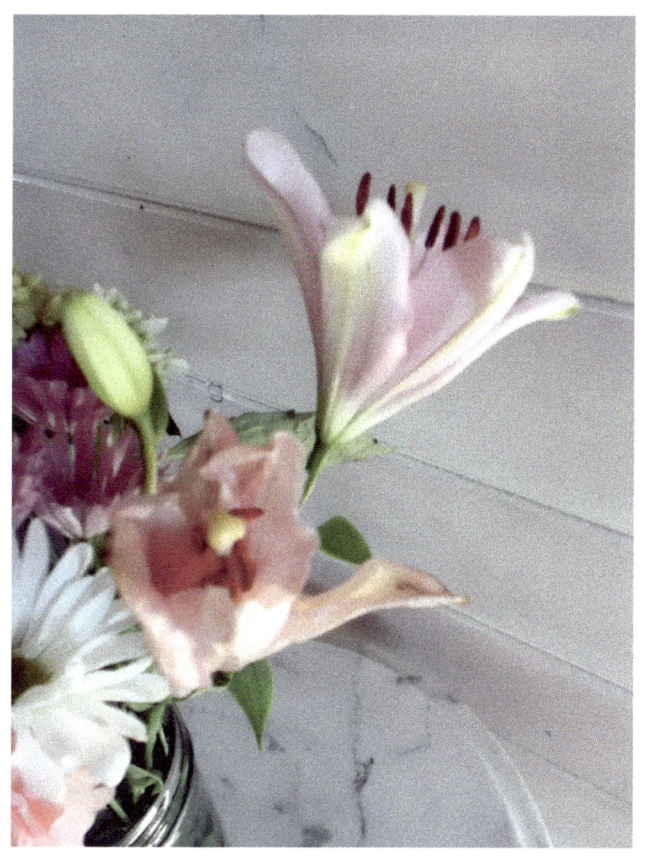

An exquisite, romanticized little ballerina.

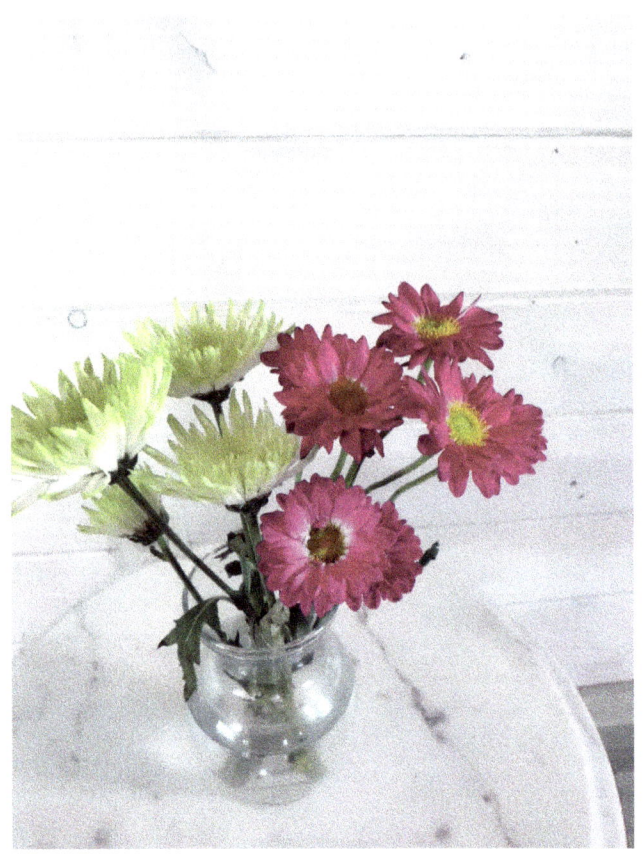

Nevertheless, the bright little apples of her cheeks, the blue of the Zuyder Zee in her eyes, the braided strands of golden corn on the wide forehead, testified to the purity of her origin. She was the school beauty.

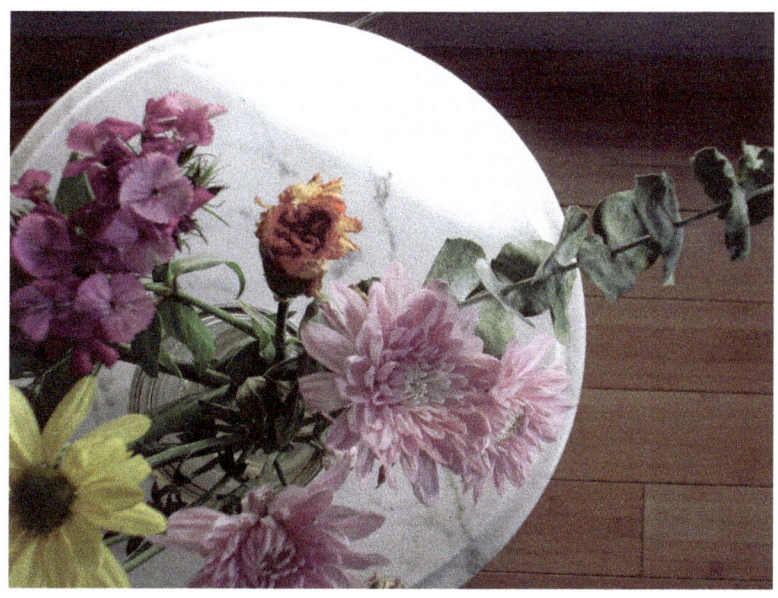

She was the girl from foreign places; she was so asleep that you could see the dream of those places in the faint lift of her forehead. He struck the inevitable creaky strip and promptly the map of wonderland written on the surface of women's eyebrows creased into invisibility.

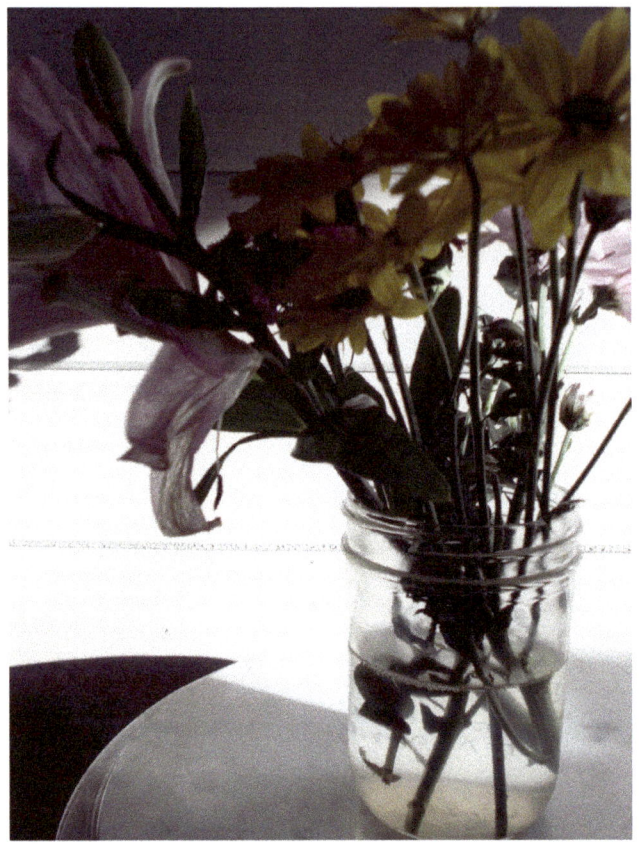

Popularly known as the "Death Ray." She was an odd little beauty with a skull-like face and hair that was a natural green-gold—the hair of a bronze statue by sunset.

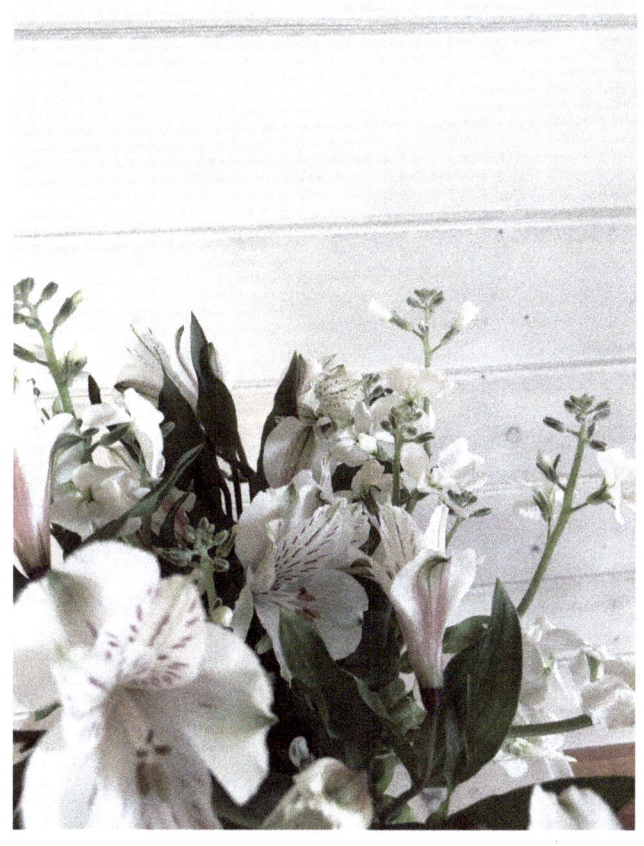

A square-chinned, decided girl with fleshy white arms and a white dress that reminded Basil domestically of the lacy pants that blew among the laundry in the yard.

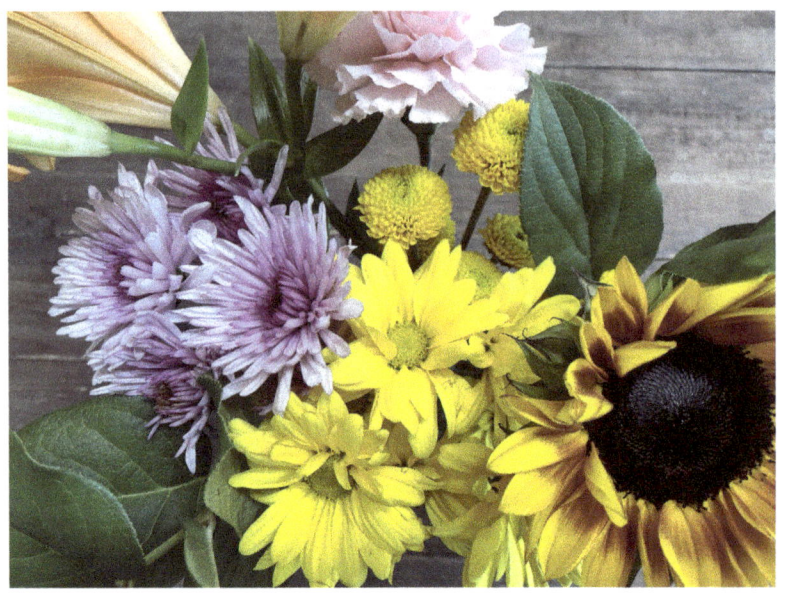

Her body was sturdy, athletic; her head was a bright, happy composition of curves and shadows and vivid color, with that final kinetic jolt, the element that is eventually sexual in effect, which made strangers stare at her.

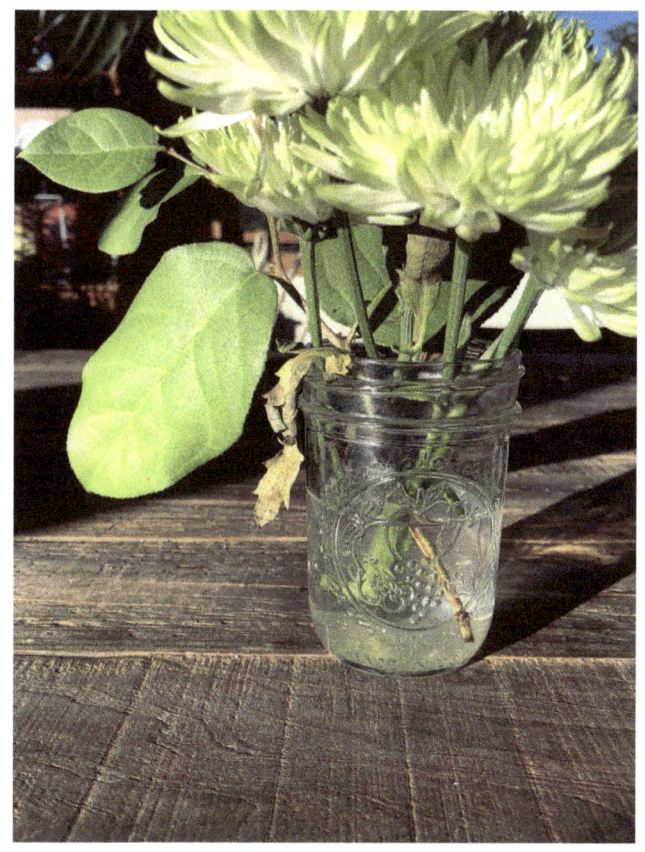

Her body was so assertively adequate that someone remarked that she always looked as if she had nothing on underneath her dress, but it was probably wrong.

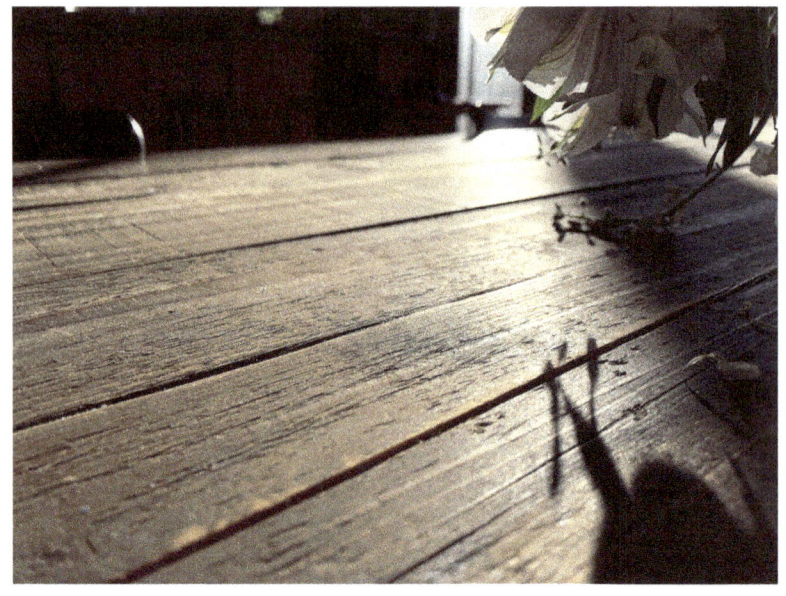

She was small with a springy walk that could have been aggressive if it had been less dainty.

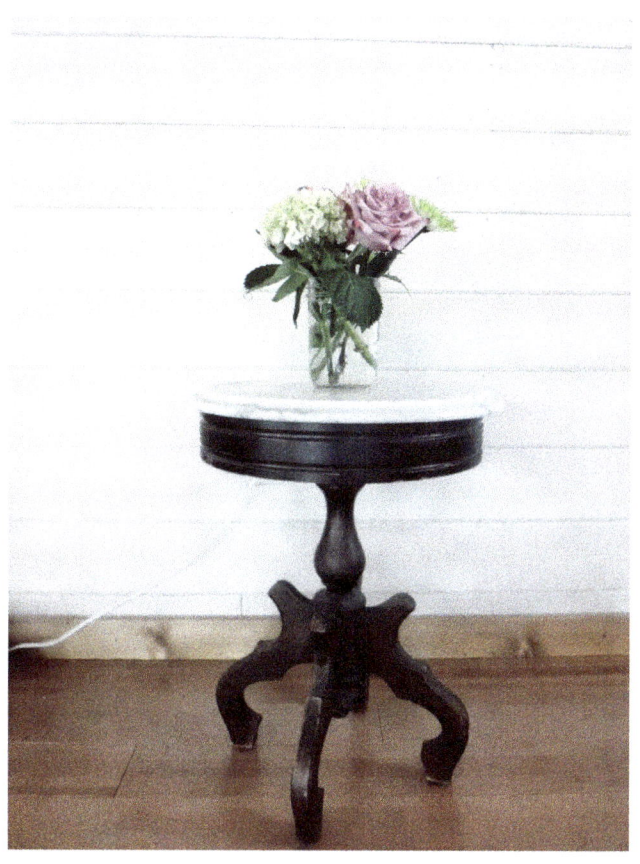

After a certain degree of prettiness, one pretty girl is as pretty as another.

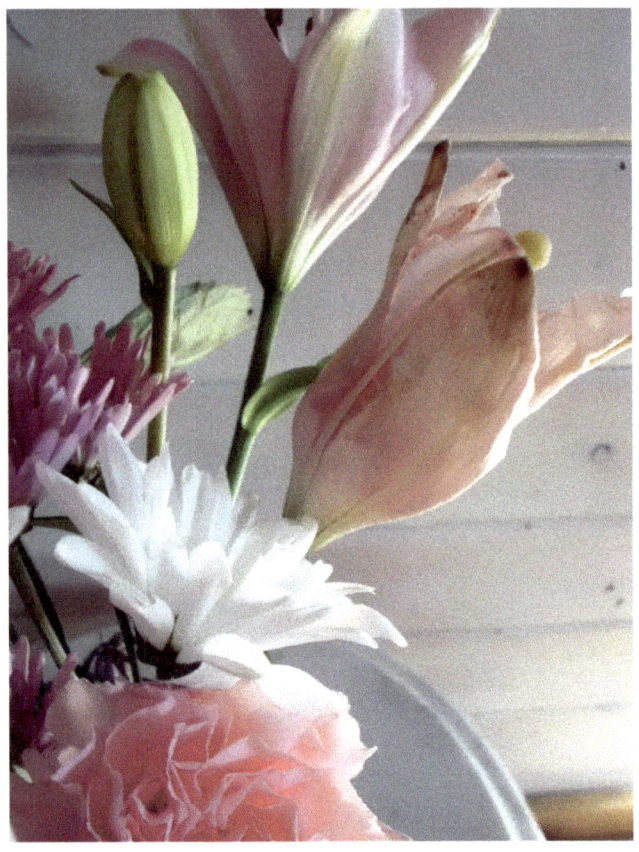

(Who has not had the excitement of seeing an apparent beauty from afar; then, after a moment, seeing that same face grow mobile and watching the beauty disappear moment by moment, as if a lovely statue had begun to walk with the meager joints of a paper doll?) Becky's beauty was the opposite of that. The facial muscles pulled her expressions into lovely smiles and frowns, disdains, gratifications and encouragements; her beauty was articulated, and expressed vividly whatever it wanted to express.

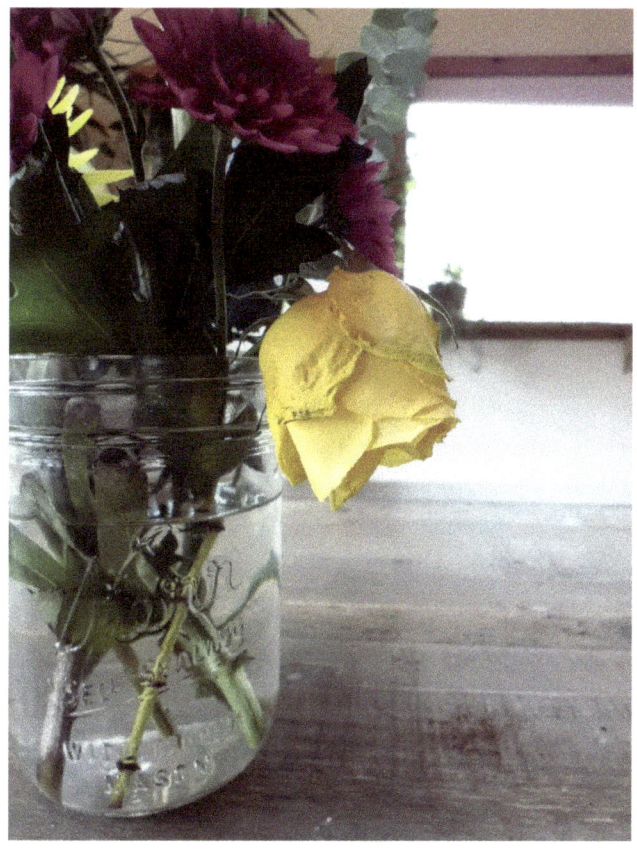

Her face was a contrast between herself looking over a frontier—and a silhouette, an outline seen from a point of view, something finished—white, polite, unpolished—it was a destiny, scarred a little with young wars, worried with old white faiths ... And out of it looked eyes so green that they were like phosphorescent marbles, so green that the scarcely dry clay of the face seemed dead beside it.

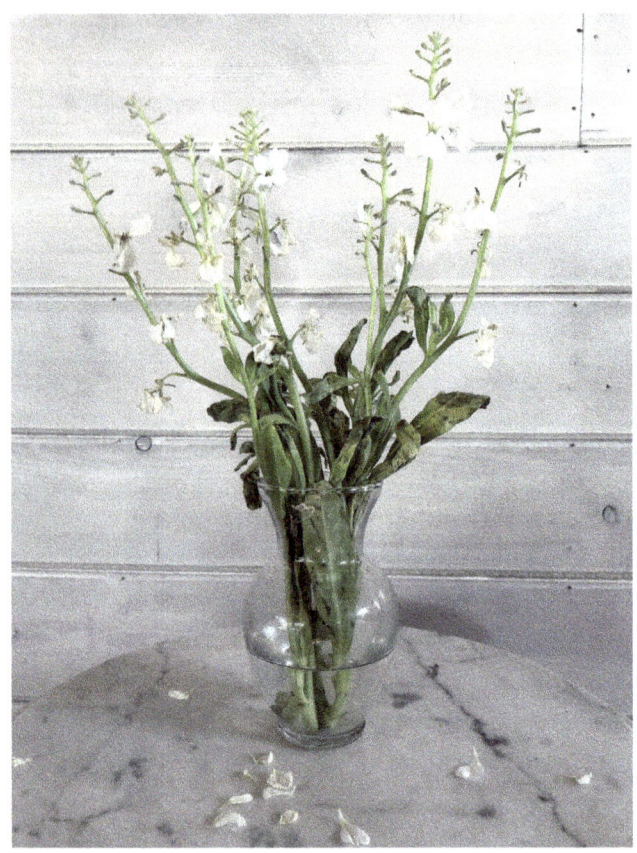

Her hair was soft as silk and faintly curling. Her hair was stiff fluff, her hair was a damp, thick shiny bank. It was not this kind or that kind, it was all hair.

    Her mouth was (different things about her mouth, contrary things, impossible to reconcile—and always with:) It was not this kind or that kind of mouth, it was all mouths.

    Also nose, eyes, legs, etc., same ending.

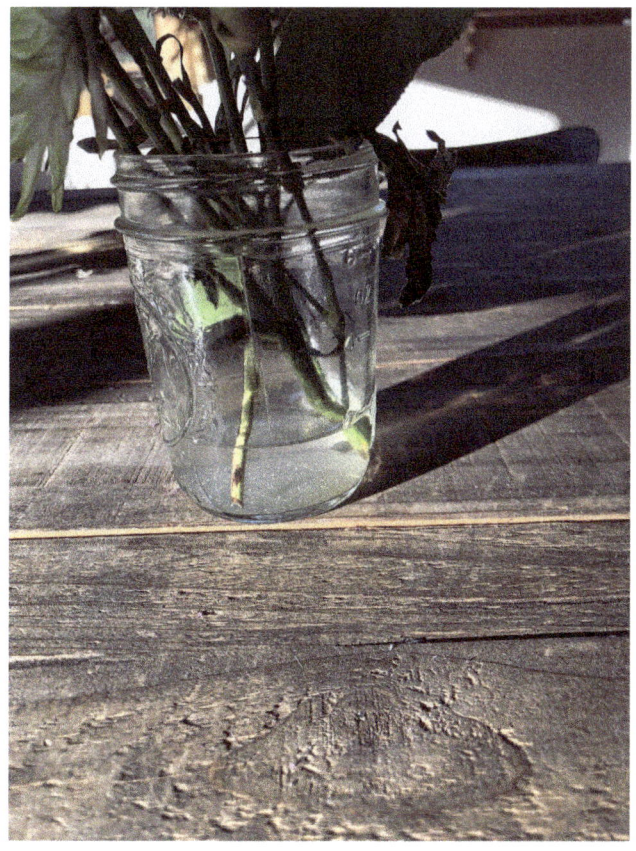

Sat a gold-and-ivory little beauty with dark eyes and a moving childish smile that was like all the lost youth in the world.

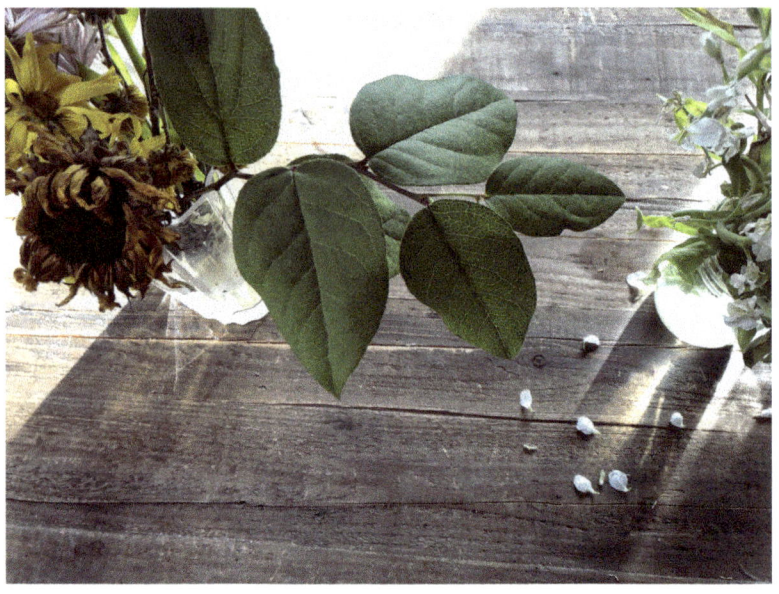

Anyone looking at her then, at her mouth which was simply a kiss seen very close up, at her head that was a gorgeous detail escaped from the corner of painting, not mere formal beauty but the beholder's unique discovery, so that it evoked different dreams to every man, of the mother, of the nurse, of the lost childish sweetheart or whatever had formed his first conception of beauty—anyone looking at her would have conceded her a bisque on her last remark.

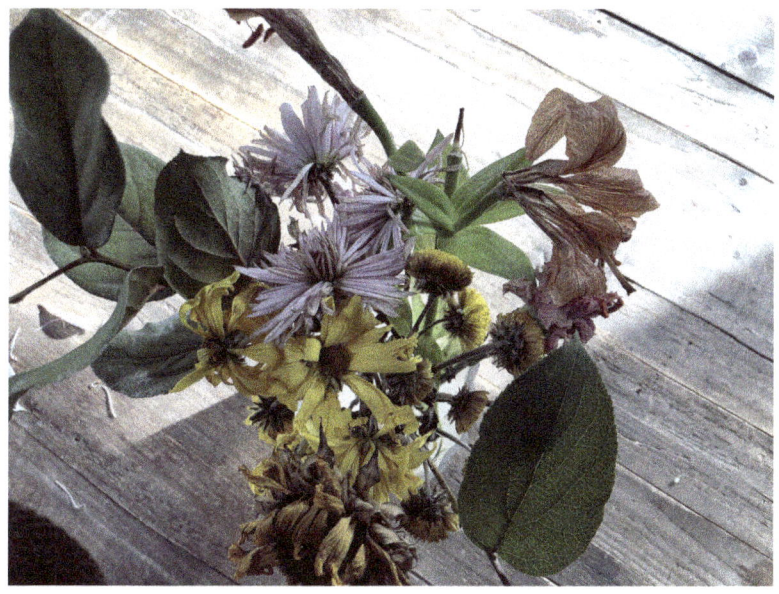

Half an hour later, sitting a few feet from the judgement dais, he saw a girl detach herself from a group who were approaching it in threes—it was a girl in a white evening dress with red gold hair and under it a face so brave and tragic that it seemed that every eye in the packed hall must be fixed and concentrated on its merest adventures, the faintest impression upon her heart.

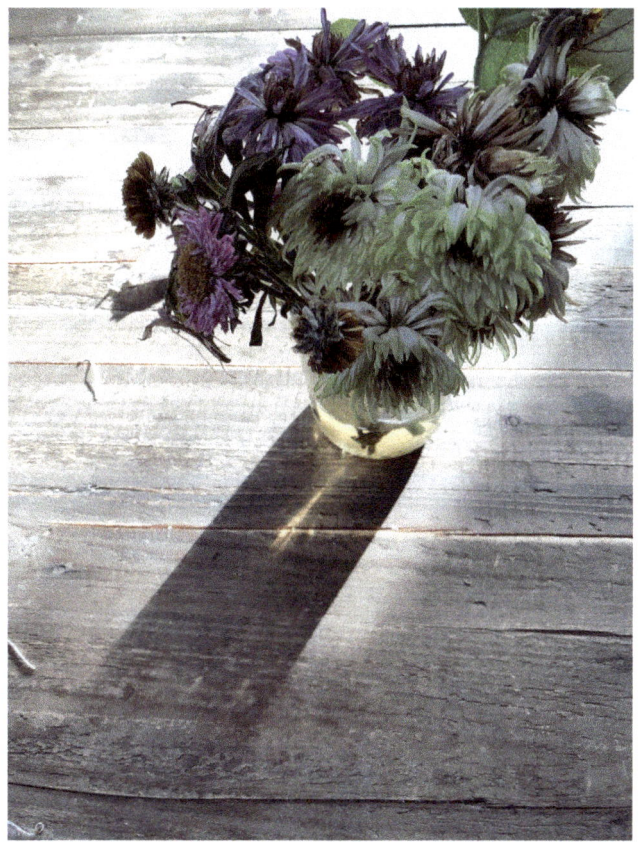

Her face, flowing out into the world under an amazing Bersaglieri bonnet, was epicene; as they disembarked at the hotel the sight of her provoked a curious sigh-like sound from a dense mass of women and girls who packed the sidewalk for a glimpse of her, and Bill realized that her position, her achievement, however transient and fortuitous, was neither a little thing nor an inheritance. She was beauty for a hundred afternoons, its incarnation in millions of aspiring or fading lives.

Birds

I

All similes and allegories concerning
her began and ended with birds.

        —Thomas Hardy

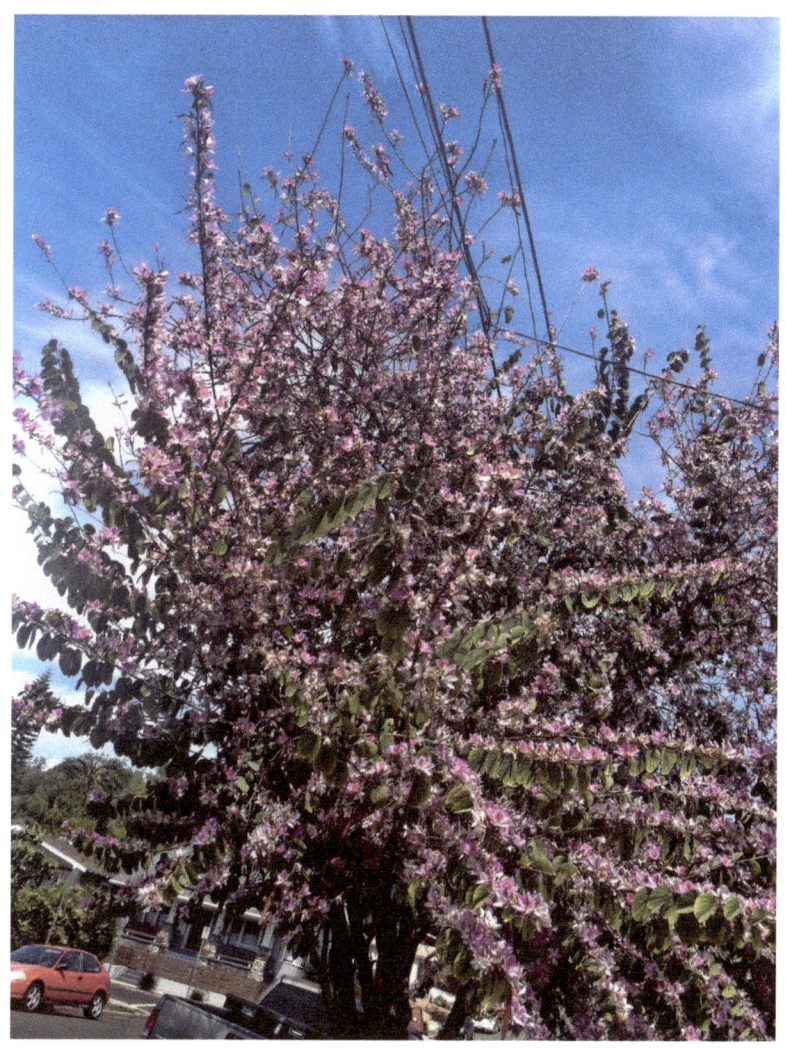

Hard flat voices.
Little chirps.
Clanking metal sheet pans and gossip.
Something will come of it.
Keep trying.

A girl in a black felt coat fumbles with her change. Slender legs in dark tights. What exactly do you expect? Or another girl, slim vintage dress. How youth glows in its random pockets of space. She stands too near you in the foyer, checking her phone, tyranical—almost violent—in her indifference.

A girl, barefoot.
Nausea.
An old man in a clean and ironed blue shirt.
Sunshine, autumn.

SOMETHING.
A girl with big brown eyes, pale face.

The girl said:
The house was flooding with oatmeal. Barack Obama was there with his little baby. I started laying hot dog buns all over the couch, then the hot dog buns got wet. I was freaking out.

The boyfriend appears, he evacuates her. He is a stale thing gone numb over centuries and the sound of her tugs at his empty agency; she grows desperate. You want to tell her. She begs, *Would you like to go somewhere else?*

You saw her: She was huge before, in her silence behind her silver fence, being anything, on the far edge of a room. The intelligence was natural but it hit the rocks. There was drama at the time; later you see it was dull drama lit up. In the photograph the light blurs everything around the rows of glasses on the windowsill.

He is at a loss.
Chirp, chirp, chirp.
Sadness settles.
A lighting up she is against heavy atmosphere. She watches him. Keeps trying, subsides. Tries again.

You want to tell her it doesn't have to be like this.

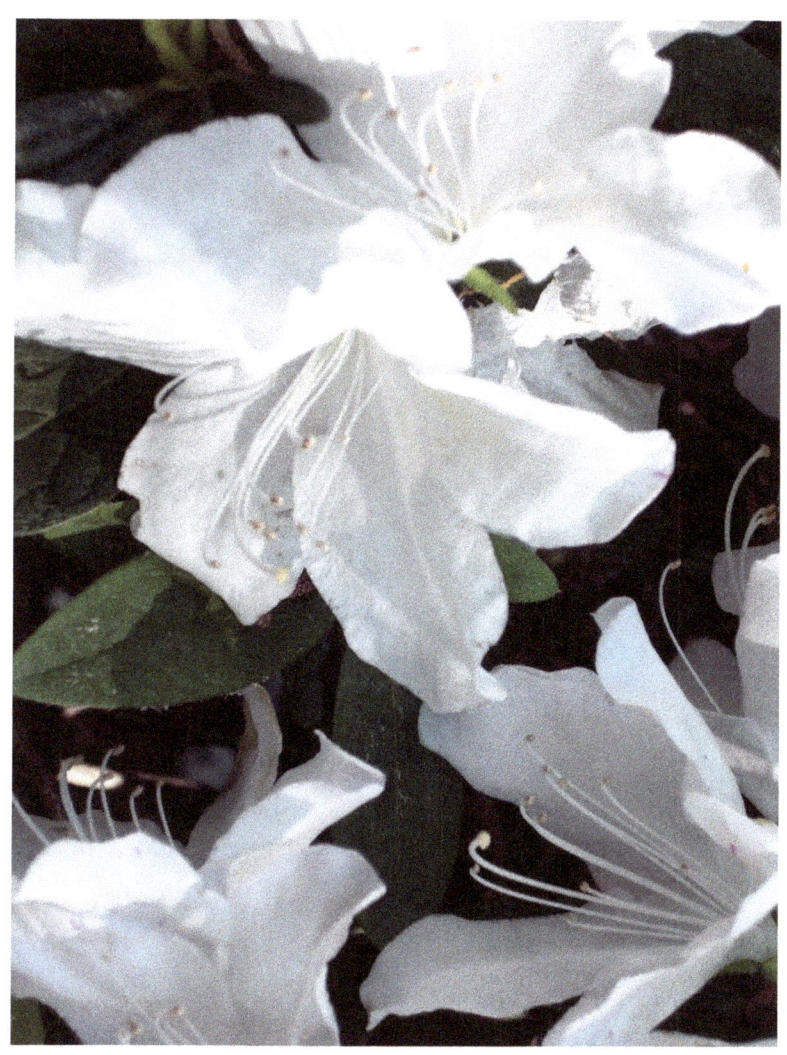

NOTHING.
The space between the sounds.

A small bird is everything and then it is gone.

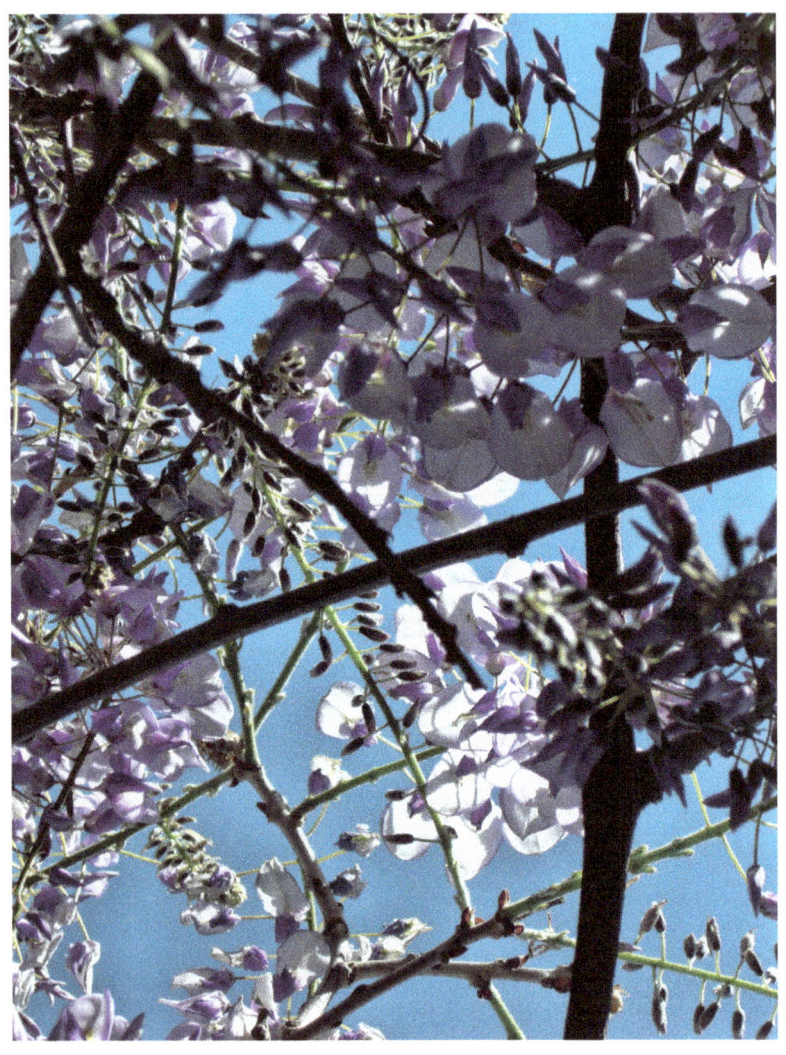

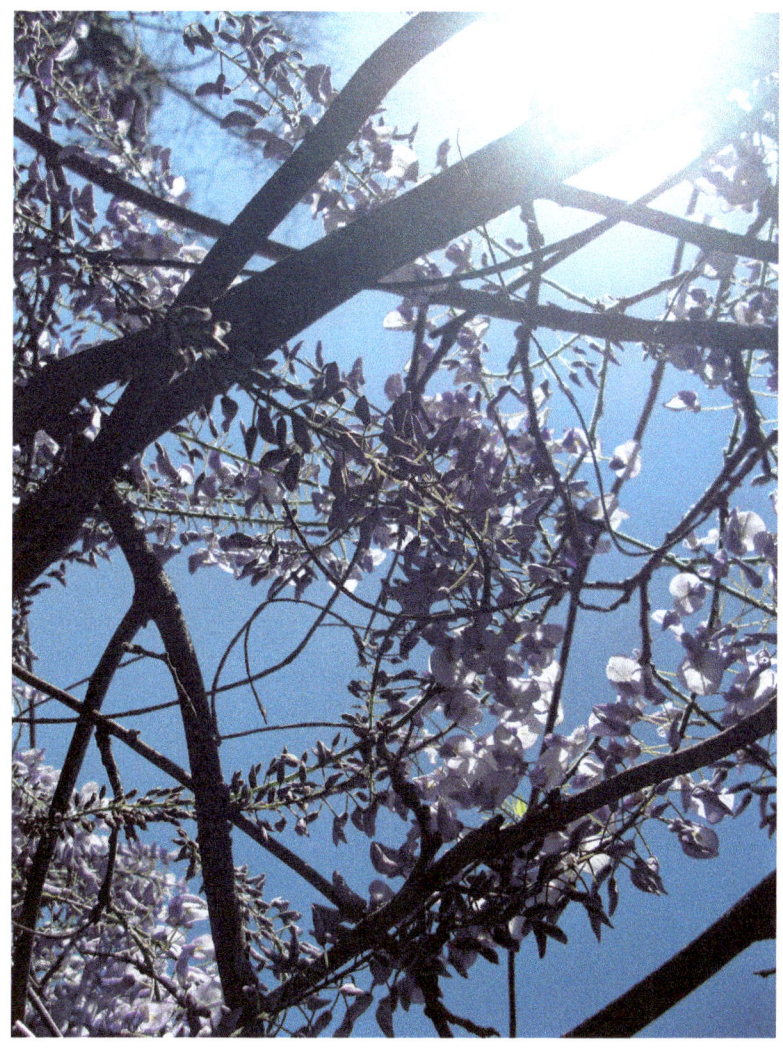

She is like a jar with another jar inside with a lid on it.

She is a world of protective iconography. Her legs are swarming with tigers; she has birds on her feet and Indian chieftains down either arm.

She is a taut package, a shell made hard. That drive means something but what exactly?

She is a bird-girl, she hunches over herself, her slenderness a diminishment, not a discipline.

She is perfect and strong in her limbs like a swimmer and her face is precocious and difficult to look at.

She is a bowl of enormous white wedding roses.

She is all smiles.

She is a whole other species for all she hasn't yet known.

She speaks as if filled with experiences long neglected by others.

She speaks as if in a television show that no one else will quite play along with.

She chatters and moves and moves and chatters, making a world of the surface of things.

She speaks as if words were stones lined up.

She speaks as if her words must first push through an enormous empty chamber within. From time to time, her voice dips into some low-pitched phrase of her father's.

She speaks within cages of her own making.

She talks and talks and talks at the coffee counter.

She covers over real peculiarities with false ones she considers to be less revealing.

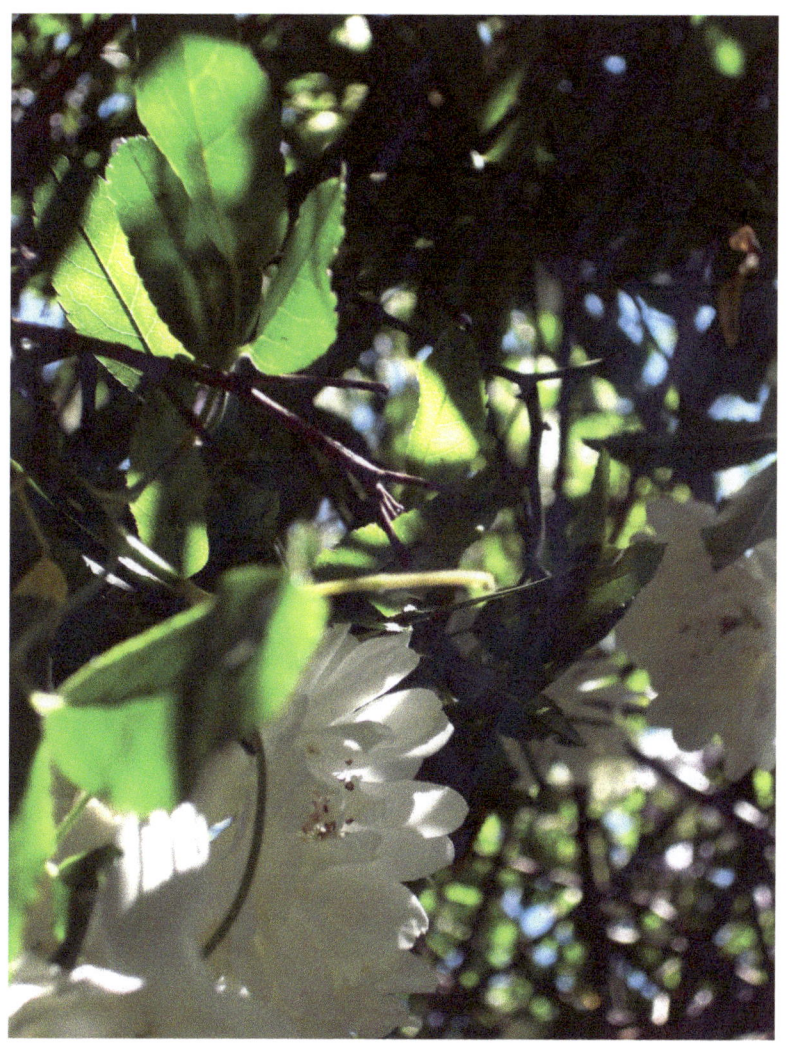

II

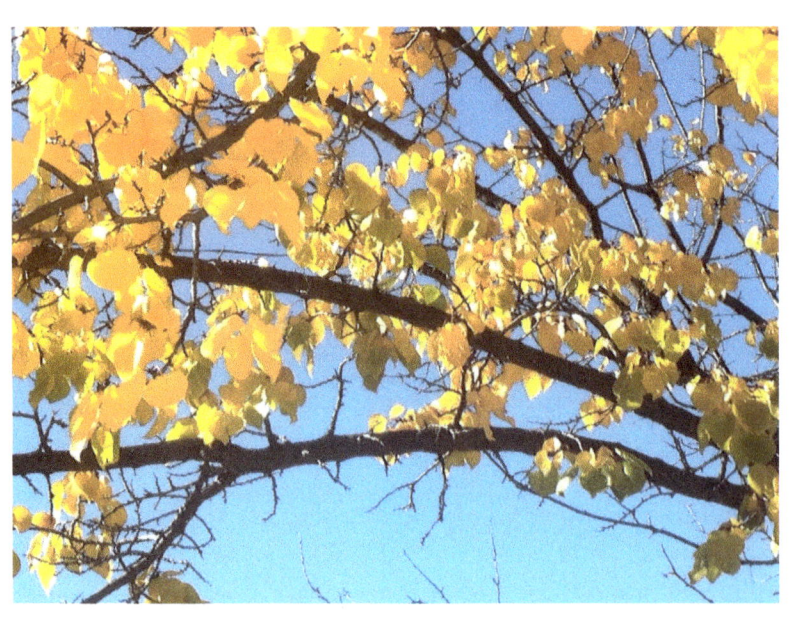

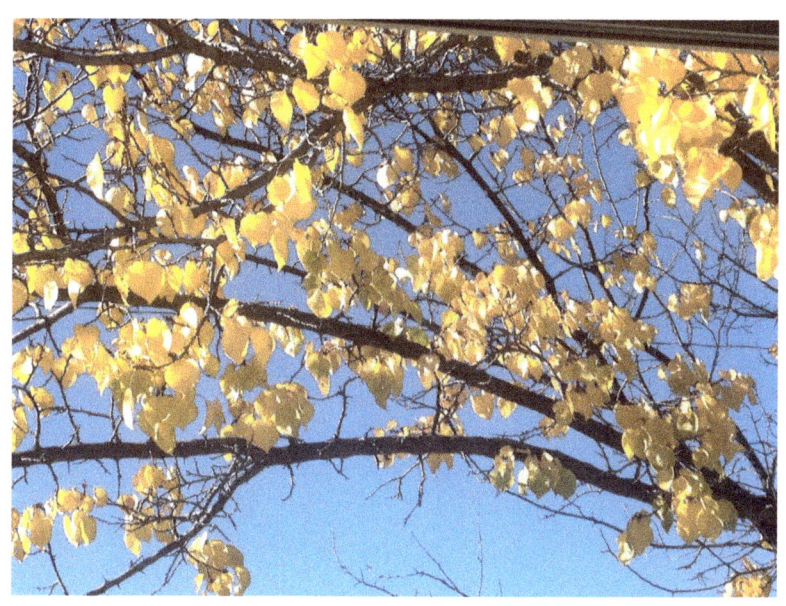

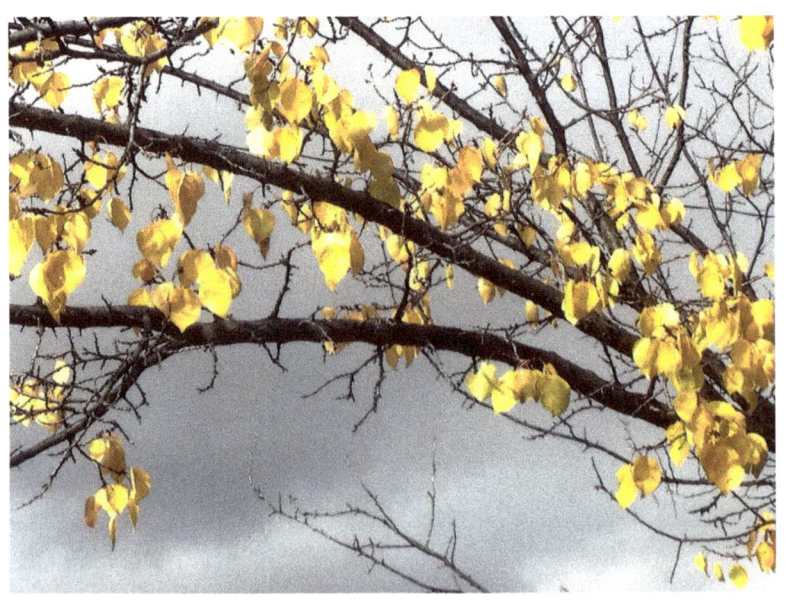

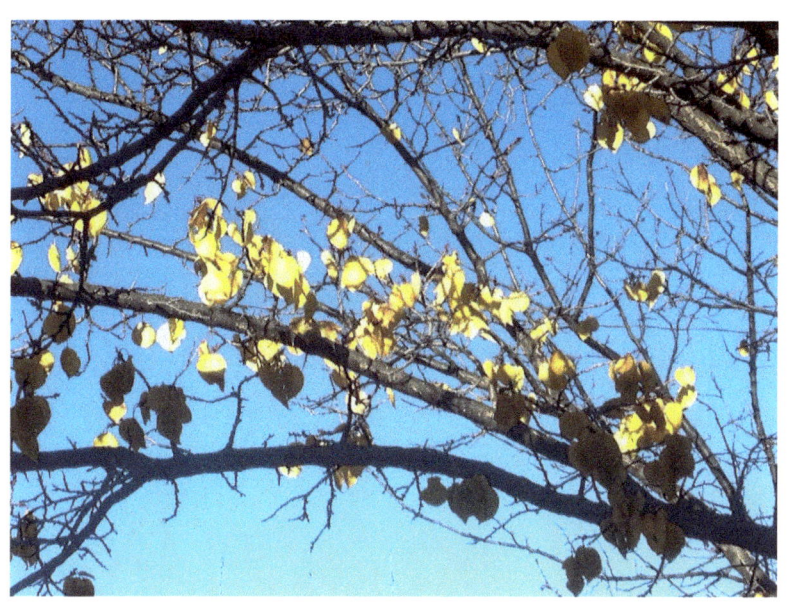

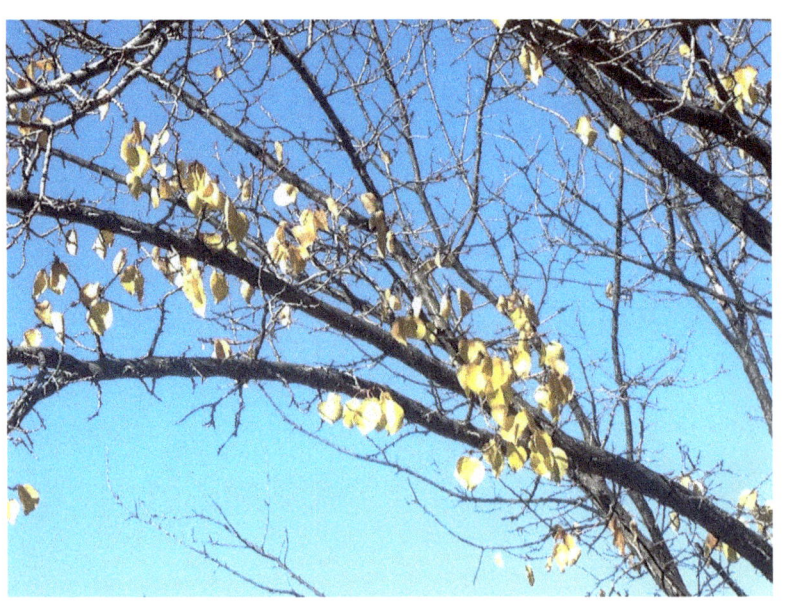

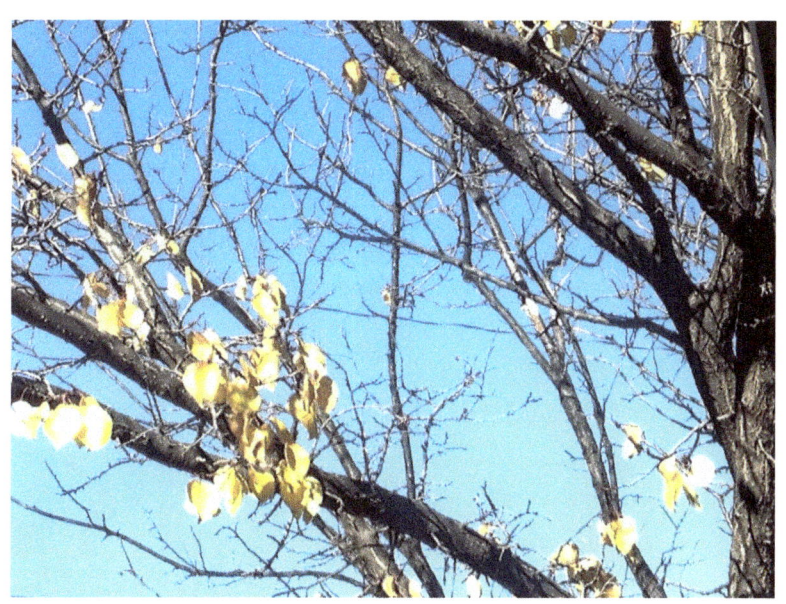

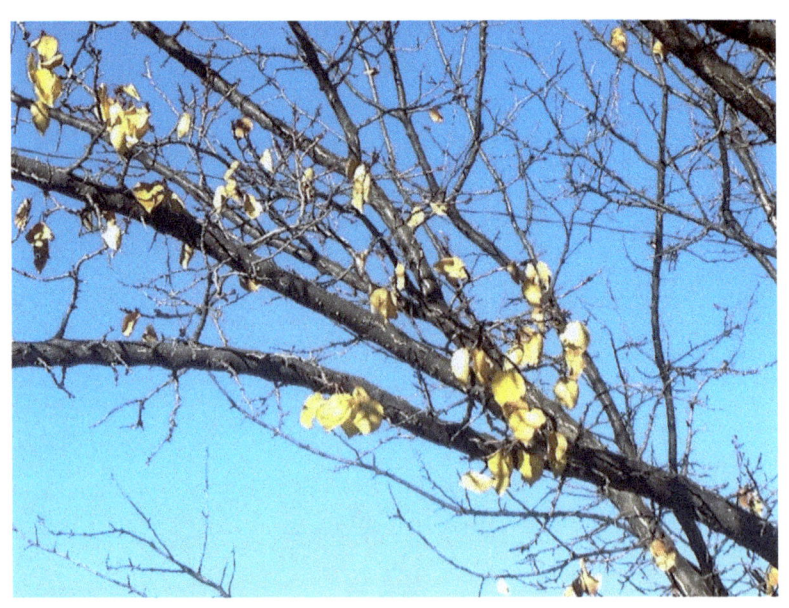

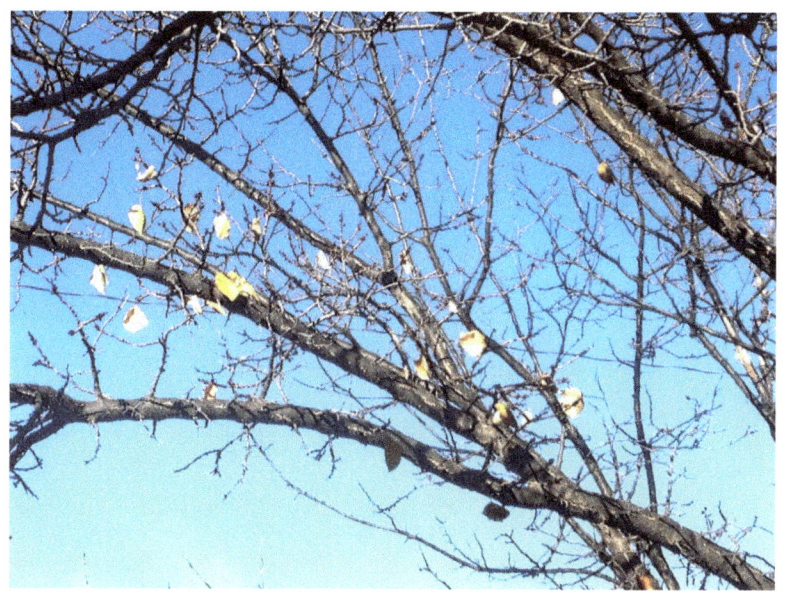

III

She dreaded with a shrinking that was scarcely sane the ridicule of the world.

—Virginia Woolf

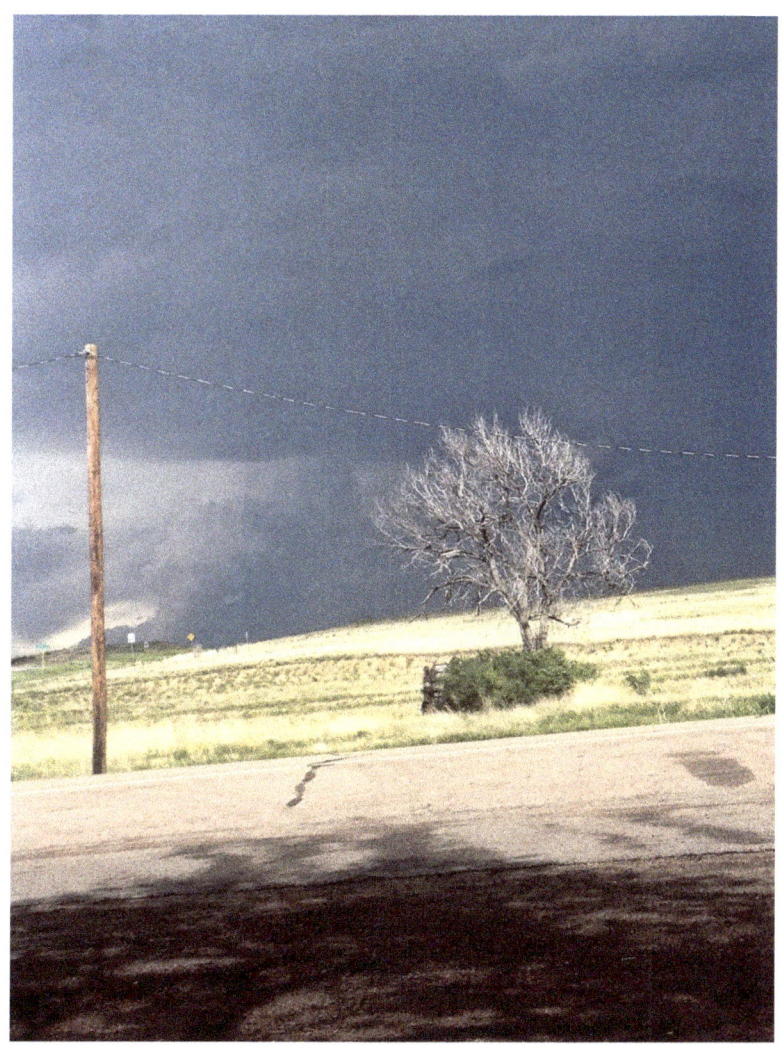

A woman buys four plastic pumpkins at a discount, slow drifting through the aisles. Old women with shopping carts, midafternoon.

Restored to a reasonable relationship with the world through an ignoble escape of its terms.

Since childhood she showed a perverse behavior, habitually poisoning street dogs.

The white haired woman every Sunday with the *New York Times* alone at the communal table, section after section, methodical, intent. Turtle-like, somewhat, in the noise of the cafe (bustling fabrics and youth and coffee sounds and laptops, dates and families and students and friends, couples who've just made love and showered). She speaks to no one, needs no one, exists nowhere else when she leaves this room. She frowns over her breakfast: the world and its obscenities. She shakes her head very slightly and nobody sees. Power abused. Resources squandered; the earth, it suffers. People suffer. Every Sunday, librarian to the world, overseer to this index of misery and folly. When done with the paper, she reads Shakespeare in paperback.*

Space curves around her. In irrelevance, everything. Complete privacy.

* This is true.

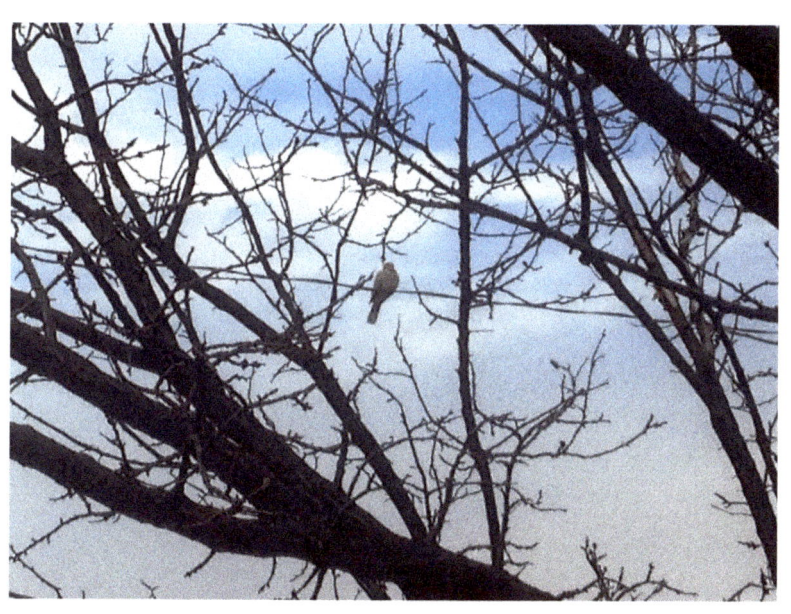

She was described as a "remarkable woman," who was "attractive in face, manner and figure, and was a fine musician." She was also intelligent. She was described to have a normal childhood, for which her mother could not recall her as having "ever said an immodest word." After puberty, she grew "more and more unnatural and strange" and led a troubled youth, leaving and returning to school at her whim. When in school, she did well in her studies.

The "form of her disease was mania, which was manifested by excitement, irascibility, incoherence of speech and violent conduct."

By May, the attending physcian indicated, she appeared better.

A vision.
A beauty.
A sight for sore eyes.

They are always blooming somewhere; it's no miracle.

But the old women at the fabric store, a colony of knowledge. Slow drift. Long gone. No one is looking or thinks to look or would ever care to look. (That old bird.) Sorting through the junk, shelves, shelves, piles, so much junk!, clearance aisle, deep discounts, HUGE end of summer deals, as a whole economic system falls to pieces. Jack-o'-lantern prints. Fleeces and jerseys. Unicorns and sports team logos and fishing rods and wine bottles and cowboys and Christmas trees. Pouring over patterns and tools.

There are real skills, and near to the skin: blankets and pillows. Toddler dresses. Wedding dresses. Controlling of experience; controlling of shape and light: curtains. Retrieving from the wreckage. From your wreckage. Conceiving long in advance and in private of effect. Salvage. Gossip. Assembly.

Where you are tender and vulnerable without knowing it.

"Caused by some disease peculiar to females."

She predicted her husband's death with astonishing accuracy. She knitted her own mourning hat as she sat at his bedside and asked her landlady's permission to store a bargain coffin in the basement.

She had a passion for death beds.

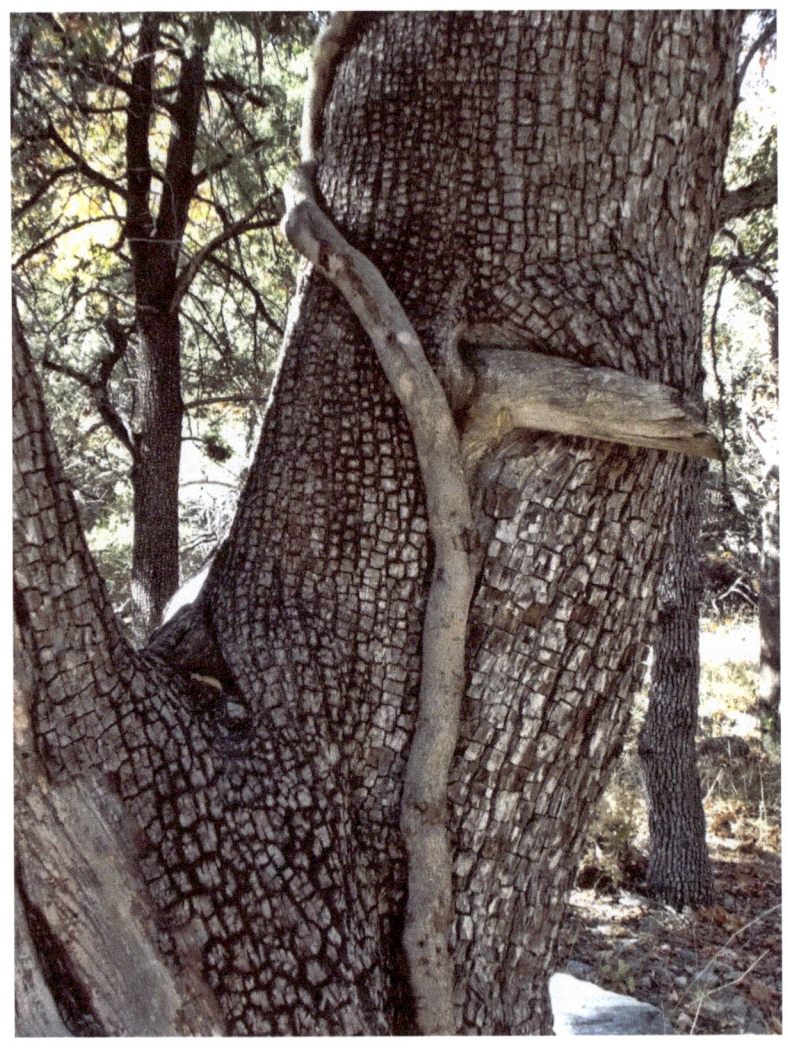

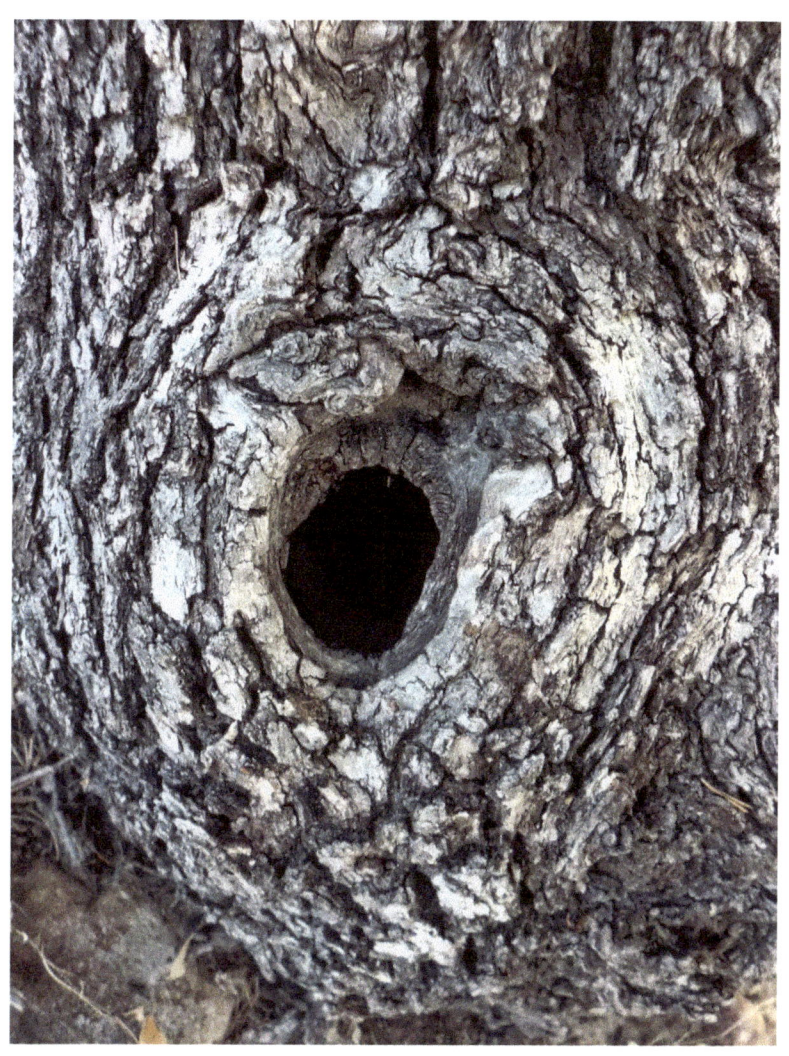

A woman's tool: like language, like beauty, like a clean surface, like fabric, like food. *There now love, sweetheart, sweet thing. Darling.* Mercy or misplaced mercy or revenge, maybe pleasure. Greed. Love. Relief. Whisper tones. Private spaces. Mothers, nurses, wives, lovers. Breath and liquids. A whole history.

"You have to trust your wife. She has her things to do, and as long as she gets them done, you don't ask questions."

It is as if once they start they find it easy.

(daughter of her first husband's sister) (her first husband) (her mother-in-law) (her daughter) (infant son of her first husband's sister) (daughter of a relative) (daughter of her second marriage) (an unnamed infant)

(her first husband) (her mother) (her daughter) (her daughter) (her father) (her son) (her brother) (her second husband) (her fiance) (her music teacher and friend) (her neighbor, friend and advisor) (her landlady) (daughter of friend) (friend, maid) (friend, creditor)

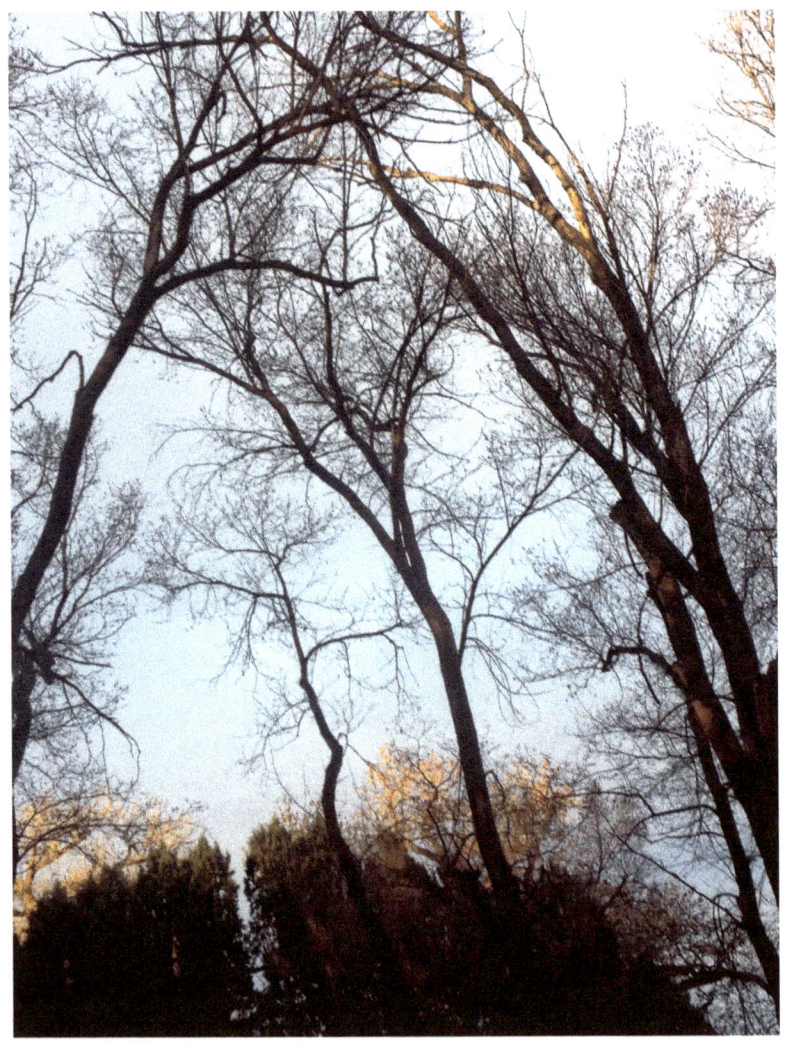

... as he threatened to prevent me from going to the west with my children, I got some more arsenic in the early part of March, through the Mitchell family, one portion which I administered to him in decoction with brandy; that is, I poured boiling water on it in a teacup, and after it had settled, mixed the water without the sediment with brandy. This mode of preparing it was intended to prevent its swimming on the surface and being discovered.

(her father) (an aunt) (her husband) (her husband) (a lover)

(husbands) (fiancés) (her mother)

(her husband) (male lover) (female customers)

(her husband) (two former lovers) (two other men)

(her four babies)

(her six children)

(her husband) (her four children)

(eight of her own children) (seven stepchildren) (her mother) (three husbands) (a lover) (an inconvenient friend)

Her own daughter, Delia, on her first birthday.

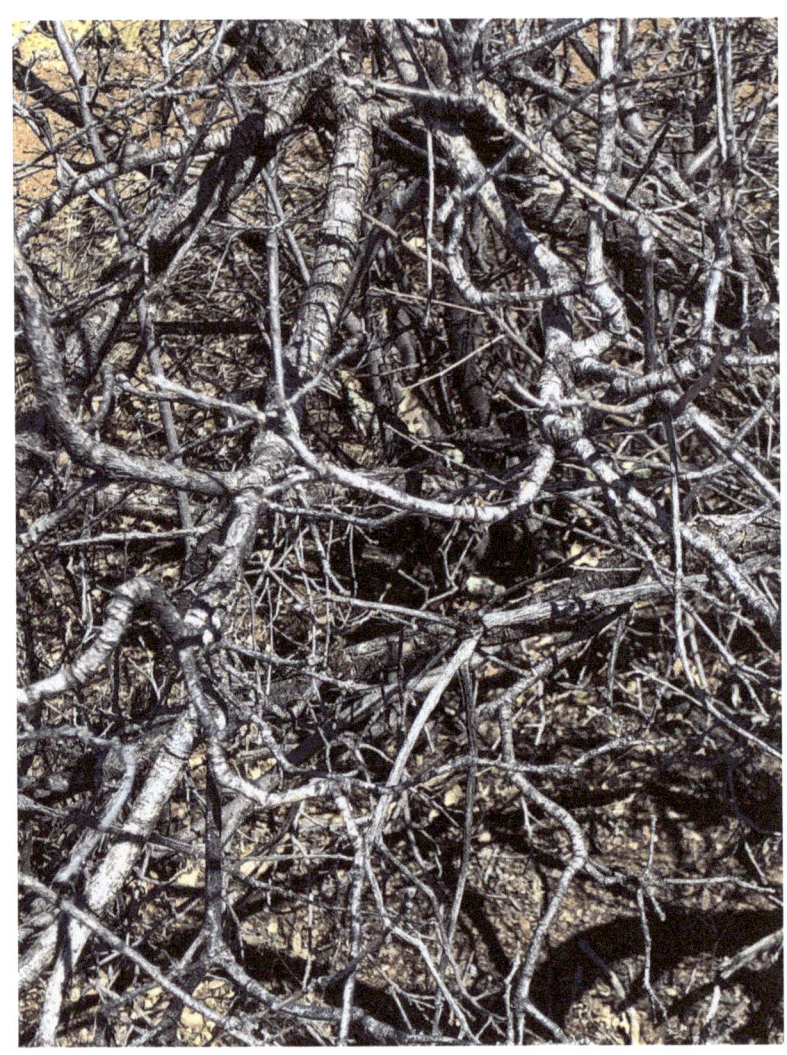

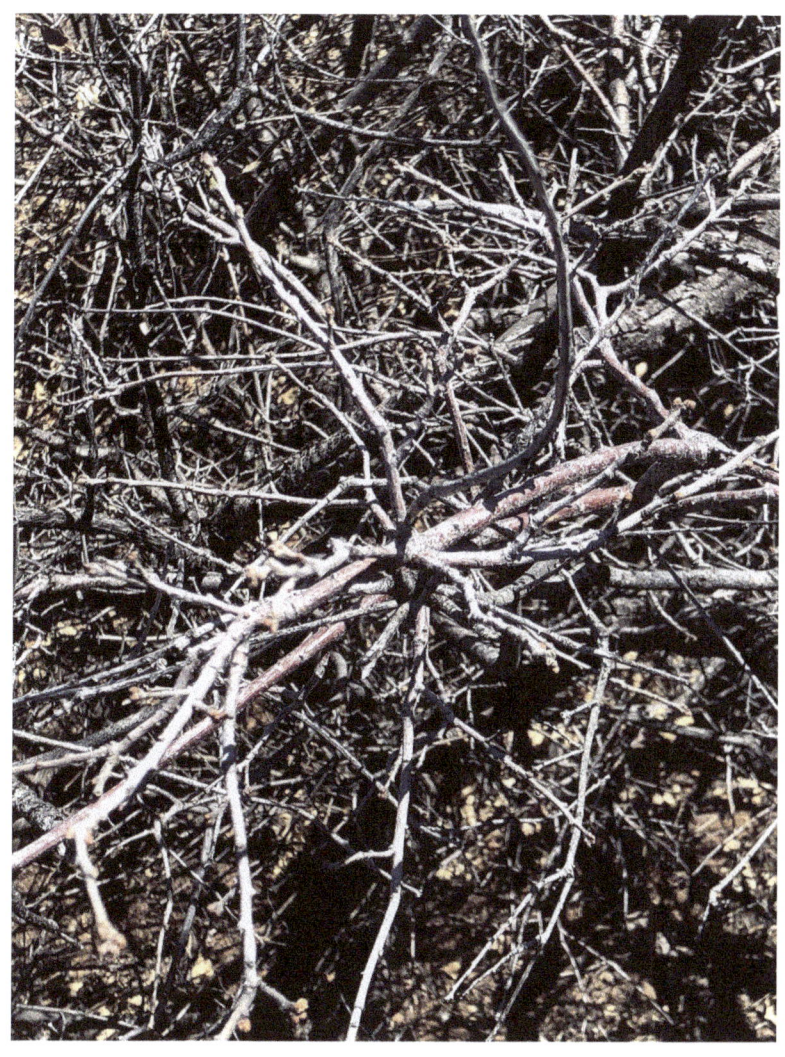

Known in her community for her cooking skills and caring for sick neighbors and relatives, [she] was arrested at Eureka, Missouri, and charged with the murders of three people.

*

Taking full advantages of her lovely face, sweet voice and good command of medicine, [she] tried to make friends with rich people, and then fooled them into drinking water or eating foods containing cyanide, the paper said.

*

[She] was known for her nurturing tonics and nutritional meals at her private nursing home in Windsor, Connecticut. [She] married and killed five elderly men. She also poisoned nine elderly women after convincing them to name her in their wills.

*

She was found to be criminally insane and was sent to State Hospital in Farmington, Missouri, where it was said she was a cook.

A Pinellas County nurse who was the night supervisor when twelve of her patients at a St. Petersburg nursing home fell ill and died.

A Nebraska woman.
A remarkable woman.
A fat, unfeeling woman.
A pretty and much-courted little woman, with a fascinating air of child-like innocence.

A Schenectady County woman who lost all nine of her children to mysterious causes. The first died legitimately of meningitus, without ever leaving the world of the hospital. (What part did that fracture?) The others she returned to the hospital like offerings, over years. She appeared with the children in her arms, one after another. When they were revived, she brought them back again dead. No one doubted her.

"Doctors found nothing medically wrong."
"Again, there seemed to be no explanation for his death."
"The doctors could find no valid medical reason why the baby simply stopped breathing."
"Officers closed their file on the case after a brief consultation with hospital physicians."

She was born in a small town. She was a nurse's aid. She tried to kill herself several times as a child.

My terror was so great at the effects produced upon him.

"I had a feeling of elation and happiness."

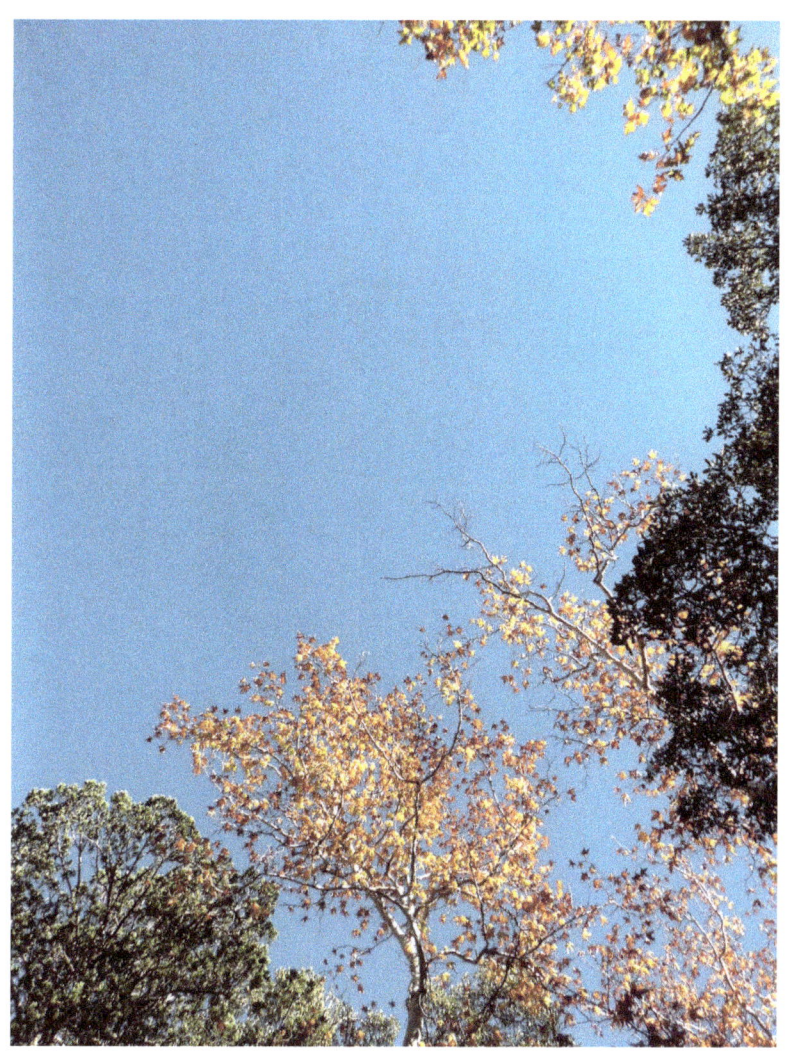

IV

On a winnowing face, colors drift. Lipstick breaches its narrow lines. The old woman chose, herself, to die at ninety-seven. She wasn't ill. It took three weeks. She grew tiny and frail and faint and went out.

It was the second time she'd chosen to die. Eighty years earlier, there was a hillside, a lover. I imagine sunlight, grass, soft summer air. Nature goes on regardless, always, indifferent to war and human calamity. The leaves of trees rippling in the breeze. A fullness in the air, summer or spring, and light slipping through the branches in twinkling patches, shifting across the grass. She poisoned herself and her lover, or he himself and her. Or both. They looked out, thinking perhaps: "What beauty this world persists in containing." They fell asleep and woke to purgatory, or worse: the prodding of German soldiers. He was poisoned again, less lovingly, in Auschwitz, and for good. She, however, was not Jewish. She spoke five languages and was put to work. She remained in that purgatory for some time more, heartbroken and wild, until breaking out across the ocean.

When she died at last, it was without help—by will alone, eighty years fortified.

Note: Some of the text in *Wild Rough Country* and in the third section of *Birds* was drawn from news reports and historical accounts. The lists, in *Birds*, that are set off by parentheses—"(husbands) (fiancés) (her mother)," etc.—are lists of the victims of female murderers throughout history, drawn from Murderpedia.org. Each paragraph or cluster represents the total number of victims of one individual woman.

www.ingramcontent.com/pod-product-compliance
Lightning Source LLC
Chambersburg PA
CBHW040521220526
45473CB00013B/2939